A LITTLE DAILY
WISDOM

A LITTLE
DAILY WISDOM

christian women mystics

carmen acevedo butcher
foreword by phyllis tickle

PARACLETE PRESS
BREWSTER, MASSACHUSETTS

A Little Daily Wisdom: Christian Women Mystics
2008 First Printing This Edition

© 2005, 2008 by Carmen Acevedo Butcher

ISBN 978-1-55725-586-0

"light" © 1993 by Lucille Clifton
Reprinted with the permission of Copper Canyon Press,
P. O. Box 271, Port Townsend, WA 98368.

All Scripture quotations are taken from the *HOLY BIBLE, NEW INTERNATIONAL VERSION. NIV* Copyright © 1973, 1978, 1984 International Bible Society. Used by permission of Zondervan Publishing House. All rights reserved.

Originally published in 2005 by Paraclete Press as *Incandescence: 365 Readings with Women Mystics* and cataloged by The Library of Congress as follows:

Library of Congress Cataloging-in-Publication Data

Incandescence : 365 readings with women mystics / [compiled by] Carmen Acevedo Butcher.
     p. cm.
  Includes bibliographical references.
  ISBN 1-55725-418-4
  1. Mysticism–Catholic Church. 2. Women mystics. 3. Spiritual life–Catholic Church. 4. Devotional calendars. I. Butcher, Carmen Acevedo. II. Title.

  BV5082.3.I53 2005
  248.2'2–dc22   2004026237

10 9 8 7 6 5 4 3 2 1

Published by Paraclete Press
Brewster, Massachusetts
www.paracletepress.com

Printed in the United States of America.

for my mother
Doris Griffin Acevedo

whose light shines

LIGHT

ray
stream
gleam
beam
sun
glow
flicker
shine
lucid
spark
scintilla
flash
blaze
flame
fire
serene
luciferous
lightning bolt
luster
shimmer
glisten
gloss
brightness
brilliance
splendor
sheen
dazzle
sparkle
luminous
reflection
kindle
illuminate
brighten
glorious
radiate
radiant
splendid
clarify
clear

ROGET'S THESAURUS

Lucille Clifton
The Book of Light

contents

foreword

*O*ne of the most poignant—by which I mean to suggest not sentimentality, but a sorrow of great dignity and a loss without remedy . . . One of the most poignant stories in American literature has to do with the poet Henry Wadsworth Longfellow. In 1841, Longfellow, a widower but still a young man, married the love of his life, Frances Appleton. The marriage was a famously happy one; and the Longfellow home, a gathering place for young and old alike. The five Longfellow children filled Craigie House with their own turmoil, while Longfellow's Harvard colleagues and students daily added a considerable amount of activity of their own. Then in 1861, while she was alone in the kitchen, sealing locks of her children's hair into waxed boxes in order to preserve them, and while the poet was working in his nearby study, Frances Longfellow somehow spilled her vat of hot wax onto the stove. Fire shot up everywhere, engulfing her in flames, and she died a few minutes later in her husband's scorched, blistered arms.

Mourning usually tempers itself, or else it succumbs to the distractions and removal of time; but that surcease did not happen for Longfellow. Finally, unable to find relief from his agony, yet no longer able to sustain it, he did what many another bereaved human being has done. He determined to distract himself by intentionally setting himself some task that, being just slightly beyond the range of his natural abilities, would exhaust him into rest . . . which is how Henry Wadsworth Longfellow came to render the most daunting poem in the Western tradition into the vernacular of the West's newest nation-state. He set himself the task of translating Dante's *Divine Comedy* for Americans.

When the work of translation was done and when, mercifully, torment had begun to soften into sorrow, the poet had only one task left before releasing the manuscript to publication. He lacked a foreword or, as he came to call it, a prologue. Forewords, by whatever name, must satisfy the fixed expectation of setting a context for the material the reader is about to read and of offering a kind of seductive precis of what lies ahead. Longfellow could do neither; the wound was too deep and the remedy he had sought too near. Instead, he wrote a sonnet, one of the most perfectly fashioned in all of American poetry, in which he describes his coming each day into the work of the *Divine Comedy* as having been an act of catharsis and devotional escape, like unto that of the spent worker who enters a cathedral at midday for respite and healing. He wrote:

Oft have I seen at some cathedral door
A laborer, pausing in the dust and heat,
Lay down his burden, and with reverent feet
Enter, and cross himself, and on the floor
Kneel to repeat his paternoster o'er;
Far off the noises of the world retreat;
The loud vociferations of the street
Become an indistinguishable roar.
So as I enter here from day to day,

And leave my burden at this minster gate,
Kneeling in prayer, and not ashamed to pray,
The tumult of the time disconsolate
To inarticulate murmurs dies away,
While the eternal ages watch and wait.

Much as I have loved Longfellow's words over the decades of my life, and as frequently as I have heard them in my own heart, as well as from the mouths of others, never had I thought of them in terms of some work other than Longfellow's *Comedy*. Or I had not until I read *A Little Daily Wisdom*. Yet I was no more than halfway through these medieval women mystics whom Carmen Butcher has so reverently translated into our American idiom before I began to hear, singing through my thoughts over and over again, "Oft have I seen at some cathedral door, a laborer, pausing in the dust and heat, lay down his burden. . . . Far off the noises of the world retreat . . . [and its tumult] to inarticulate murmurs dies away, while the eternal ages watch and wait."

The circumstances surrounding the Butcher translations were very different, of course, from those surrounding Longfellow's. This time, moreover, the one speaking the words of the sonnet prologue was neither the author nor the translator of the volume in question; rather, it was I, the book's reader, who was murmuring the words to myself. But the cathedral metaphor held for me; and in my reading, the cathedral effect was there—the easing of the burden, the kneeling in prayer and not ashamed to pray, and most blessedly, the realization that the loud vociferations of the street were indeed fading away into indistinguishable sounds.

One can say—and I have said to myself several times—that the cachet of the medieval, which so drenches these mystics of Butcher's choosing, is the same that perfumes Dante's *Commedia*; for the medieval, after all, was his time and theirs, having been at best only lent to the rest of us who have followed. Or one can say that the parallels between Longfellow's americanizing intention toward a medieval classic and Carmen Butcher's are certainly there in effect, if not in cause. One can even note acerbically that cathedrals and medieval translations invite a kind of inevitable juxtaposing. But there is more than these things resonating here.

This small collection really is, in substance and in detail, a house of God where all who dare may enter. I say dare, because this house was chiseled out of life's living stone by women who worked in a time when strong women were prophets and seers of God. In these pages, the images of the Spirit's life are the erotic ones of the feminine experience. They are the stuff of very physically present women who, born in a lustier time, lived fully in the flesh and loved their Lord with a ferocity and passion that could be reported only in those experiences of the flesh. Stern mother-love also courses through these passages of adoration and exultation, as does mother-counsel. There is quiet here, too, deeply running quiet, just as there is a roar of holy fervor which suppresses and surpasses all other of the heart's roars. And then, too, there is a bit of that sly, exquisitely feminine, faintly mocking trick of seeing out of the corner of the eye and then almost—just almost—laughing about it.

Beyond all these things, though, there is peace here in the company of these good women—peace, and the nurture that only wise and well-worn priestesses can bring to a day's occupation. So it is in their name, not mine, that I invite you: enter here, and laying your burden at this minster gate, listen for a year (or a clutch of years). Then marvel with me as the noises of the world do indeed retreat into inarticulate murmurs that soon begin to die away.

PHYLLIS TICKLE

The Farm In Lucy

What makes this volume different from other devotional writings? This book is about a luminous God, who loves us as gently as a mother and knows us as well as a lover. In recent times greater numbers of people are looking for an authentic relationship with this all-powerful, incarnate deity. That's where the medieval women mystics can help us. They preach Radiance. They focus on the unconditional nature of God's love. God's incandescent mercy is far more attractive to them than the dark finger-pointing concerns of a more masculine, medieval spirituality which was often obsessed with original sin and with guilt.

Among their bright themes is the reminder that we can converse with God. Catherine de Heuck Doherty, a twentieth-century Canadian mystic, offers this classic description of what these medieval women knew so well:

> A mystic is simply a man or woman in love with God, and the Church is hungry for such people. . . . It isn't hard to be a mystic. All we have to do is fall in love with God; the rest will follow . . . the mystics of the Church call us to experience God by being in love with Him; He is already in love with us.[1]

That's why mystics make alacritous teachers. They are enthusiastic in the most essential sense of that word. They know and love "the God within," so they are original, extreme, frank, ordinary, and often eccentric, but always relevant. Their writings may sometimes seem bizarre to our smug, scientific perspective, but that's only because the spiritual world was so real to them.

Through these independent women, we experience the unfathomable serenity of God's supreme love. Their God is never faceless. They dialogue with a loving Person, not an abstract intellectual concept. God is as intimate as your own breath. His three-in-oneness is as accessible as it is mysterious. This is good news for a world constantly interacting with answering machines and automated tellers.

These medieval mystics make excellent spiritual teachers for contemporary readers, because they are risk-takers. One example suffices: On a dark night in Italy nearly eight hundred years ago, Clare Offreduccio, unable to accept her birthright—a life of privilege and an economically sensible marriage—escaped through a small side door in her family's pricey home. This runaway teenager followed the God of light to become the future St. Clare of Assisi.

These women are risk-takers in love, knowing God in ways we often do not. The immensely likeable Catherine of Siena is quick to tell us we should risk everything for God's goodness, because it is within the reach of every honest heart. She is delighted that the more you love God, the more you know God, and the more you know God, the more you want to love Him, and so on, snowballing into never-ending joy. She rejoices that agape love is addictive and that gaining godly knowledge is possible. All that it requires is a little focus. She explains, "If you want to find and experience the fruit of God's will, always live in the cell of your soul."

Being alone with yourself and learning to trust in God takes courage. But in that private soul place, these medieval women mystics meditated consistently, for hours and days and years and decades, creating the devotionals gathered and presented here, which now sparkle like diamonds. They explore the world of God's divine, mothering love, the guidance of God's light, the sensuality of faith, and a helpful Trinity.

Julian of Norwich reminds her readers that every time we make ourselves vulnerable before God, allowing a weakness to be exposed before Love, we are rewarded for this risk: "God pats us secretly, reassuring us, and showing us our sins by the gentle light of His sweet mercy and grace." The more we humble ourselves before God, the more we see that our every weakness, pain, grief, embarrassment, or harmful error is met with His divine patience and love. Julian embodies her entire theology in this sense of God's love as "meaning":

> Would you like to know your Lord's meaning?
> Okay, then know it well. The Lord's meaning is Love. Love is His only meaning.
>
> Who shows this to you? Love.
> What did He show you? Love.

And why does He show it to you? For love.

Stay in God's love, then, and you'll learn more about its unconditional, unending, joyful nature. And you'll see for yourself, all manner of things will be well.

For those of us who wonder how we will know what to risk spiritually and when to risk it, the mystics recommend divine light's illuminating presence. Marguerite d'Oingt had a vision in which she witnessed the redeeming luminescence of Christ's broken body: "From these magnificent wounds poured out a light, so great it was stunning." Christ's radiant wounds of light liberate us from our gloomy self-absorption and our own dark wounds. As Catherine of Siena tells it, "The cloud of self-centered love darkened the eye of my understanding, but You came with Your light, Eternal Trinity, and banished all the darkness in me!"

We will also be guided by the very intimacy of a growing relationship with God, as Mechthild of Magdeburg tells us in her poetry. Well-known for her love mysticism, she invites us to enjoy a sensual faith: "Lie down in the fire and see and taste the flowing Godhead in your being. Feel the Holy Spirit move in you, compelling you to love God, His fire, and His flowing in many different ways."

Catherine of Siena echoes the very physicality of faith, "Let God's light help and comfort you. Now, no more words, but action!" She reminds us that God's luminescence is a way of living: "You, God, light coals on fire with the love that eventually melts hatred and bitterness from the hearts and minds of those who are full of anger. It will even turn their hatred into tenderness."

Gertrude the Great is of the same mind: "Remember kind actions—more than anything else—cause the soul to shine with brilliance."

We need these mystics' unapologetically *feminine* view of a tender, nurturing, forgiving God, who shares the divine body with the beloved—and the beloved is, of course, everyone. This God bleeds for us and lets us suckle nourishment from the divine breast, as Catherine of Siena says:

> Love gives her children milk. Love feeds her children well.
> We get this milk in the same way a baby sucks milk from its
> mother's breast. We get our nourishment by sucking milk
> through Love's nipple. Just so, our soul can have life only
> through Christ crucified.

When these women who knew pregnancy, birthing, pain, and bleeding describe the special intimacy a maternal God offers, they are convincing. Their yearnings for close relationships with the people in their lives inform their ideas of God as the gentle, attentive Lover. Their own complex relationships as mothers, sisters, wives, and friends form the foundation of their understanding that God's love is relational. Loving God means establishing and maintaining healthy bonds with those at our elbow. Like the contemporary poet Lucille Clifton, who wrote the poem "light," their honest voices and sometimes startling visions are life-affirming.

These women challenge us from their understanding of simpatico suffering. They knew the darkest days, too, and their thoughts on depression are especially sinewy. When I was a college freshman, my roommate taped a Pollyanna-yellow poster up on her side of the room. This poster's too-bright theology bugged me. It announced, "The best prayer is one word, 'HELP!'" However—two decades later—that little word *Help!* has become a real friend, mainly because of my own encounter with the spiritual world of depression. The devotionals in this book speak to that world. Because the mystics were especially susceptible to black days, they can teach us how to say the word *Help!* and look to God for light.

In the pages that follow, seventeen famous, and not-so-famous, medieval women mystics—Hildegard of Bingen, Catherine of Siena, Gertrude of Helfta, Julian of Norwich, Catherine of Genoa, Birgitta of Sweden, Angela of Foligno, Marguerite Porete, Hadewijch of Brabant, Margery Kempe, Beatrijs of Nazareth, Elisabeth of Schönau, Mechthild of Magdeburg, Teresa of Avila, Umiltà of Faenza, Clare of Assisi, and Marguerite d'Oingt—converse with God in original ways. They invite each one of us to join in their intimate relationship with God.

A Little Daily Wisdom offers the concentrated spiritual wisdom of these mystics in easy-to-use, daily form. As a sort of mystics primer, it presents their most representative, most arresting, most convincing passages, and is intended to help readers create a "cell" or "quiet space" for focusing on God's love in the midst of busy lives. There is a meditation, a prayer, a poem or song for every day in a year's journey.

Each one is designed to be used as a private devotion. Taken into the spirit early in the morning, a medieval woman's meditation can sing to you throughout the day. Read before bed, it can put your mind to rest as you prepare for a night's sleep. The devotionals can be enjoyed back to front or front to back, one at a time, or many all at once, whichever works best for you.

My hope is that these pages will taste good to your soul, and I know that would especially please these women, because they wanted nothing more than to midwife spiritual nourishment in others. They hungered for the love, joy, peace, patience, kindness, goodness, faithfulness, gentleness, and self-control that the New Testament book of Galatians describes, and they wanted others to have these, too. Over and over, they point out that the first spiritual step is always the hardest because it requires honesty and humility.

Readers wanting to know more about these women and their spiritual pluck can find short biographical information in a separate section at the back. I hope the selected reading list also provided there will make you curious to read more about these hard-to-pigeonhole women who deserve and reward any extra study.

I've modernized the mystics' words (or, in some cases, those words written about them) so the readings will sound more familiar and appealing. Many of the passages are condensed, but I have omitted ellipses. I have also changed many third-person passages into first-person. In all these changes, my goal was to make the text more reader-friendly. I enjoyed reading many Latin and German works in the original, and labored through many Old French texts.

Being still before God is never easy, but the devotional readings in this book can make the attempt all the more worthwhile. As you spend time with these mystics, may you enjoy a dialogue with a mysterious God, who is the Light leading us out of every darkness.

---

[1]See Catherine de Heuck Doherty, preface to *Purgation and Purgatory, The Spiritual Dialogue: Catherine of Genoa*, Serge Hughes, trans. (New York: Paulist Press, 1979), pp. xiii–xiv.

january

january 1 🌿

On New Year's Day,
we hope the new season
brings new flowers and new joys.
But—come what may—
those who suffer and worry for Love
will live joyful lives.

Love's rich power is creative and friendly.
Love is kind and has a sweet temperament.
Love soothes with compensation
every new sadness.

Love knows the repeated blows
I must endure for her.
From now on, though, I'll rely on Love.
totally,
with a sad heart, joyful.

—Hadewijch, *Poems in Stanzas*—

january 2 🌿

God tells us, "You must help achieve your own salvation. Obedience is the key of the Word, but you must still use it. So walk by the light of faith, stretching out your hand in love. I created you with no help from you, without your asking Me, because I loved you—how I love you! I loved you even before you existed.

"But you must help Me save you. Carry the key in your hand. And walk—don't sit—along the way of Truth's teaching. Don't sit by the fire, concentrating on finite things and glittery material possessions. If you do, you're throwing the shiny key of obedience into manure. You're smashing it with a hammer. You're letting it get rusty with self-absorption. Instead, tie this key tight around your waist with the belt of humility and submission. Wear it with joy. Then you'll never lose the key to Love."

—Catherine of Siena, *Dialogue*—

january 3 🌿

God is a happy Trinity, and God is everlasting, a creature with no end and no beginning. His omnipresence always intended the creation of the world and of all of us who live in it, and God's sensual, beautiful character was first designed for His Son, who is the second person of the Trinity.

When the Trinity—through love—made the world and us, this act of creativity joined every one on earth to God, and this unique unity helps us stay as pure and as excellent as when we

4

were first created. In this bond with God, we are strong. In it we love and thank the One who made us.

We can't stop praising Him. God's good love is continually re-created in every soul who seeks healing in God's will.

—Julian of Norwich, *Revelations*—

january 4 🌿

A voice from heaven sang out, saying to me:

"Depressed child of God and daughter of much hard work, even though you've been thoroughly seared—so to speak—by endless terrible pains in your body, the deep mysteries of God have completely permeated you. Give others an accurate account of what you see with your inner eye and what you hear with the inner ear of your soul. Your testimony will benefit others. As a result, men and women will learn how to know their Creator, and they'll no longer refuse to adore God with excellence and respect."

That voice made me—heartbroken and fragile creature that I am—begin to write with a trembling hand, even though I was traumatized by more illnesses than I could count. As I started this task, I looked to the true and living Light and asked, "What should I write down?" I was never in a condition similar to sleep, nor was I ever in a state of spiritual bliss. I saw the visions with the inner eye of my spirit and grasped them with my inner ear.

—Hildegard of Bingen, *Book of Divine Works*—

The Holy Spirit, the Paraclete—giver of everything good—breathes where He wants and how He wants and when He wants and keeps all secret inspiration hidden, but sometimes God's Spirit decides to bring spiritual truths to light, for the good of the many. That's what happened in my case. Divine love always flowed into my servant soul, but I was only commanded to make this known on some occasions.

One Mass, as the host was being consecrated silently by the priest, I said to the Lord, "This act is so significant and so deserving of ultimate respect that in its presence I must lie down in the deepest valley of humility and there wait my portion of it bringing my salvation."

But the Lord answered me, "When a mother wants to embroider with silk or pearls, sometimes she puts her little child up in a higher place to hold the thread of pearls or to help her in other ways.

"That's why I've put you in a higher place—I intend to make you participate in this Mass. If you'll raise yourself up to help Me of your own volition in My work of love—even if it's hard—then you'll have helped Me as best you can, according to your unique abilities."

—Gertrude the Great, *The Herald of Divine Love*—

O blessed poverty,
you give everlasting wealth to all who love you!
O holy poverty,
God promises eternal glory and a joyful life to all who
possess and crave you!
O God-centered poverty,
you whom the Ruler of heaven and earth and Creator of all
that was made
—our Lord Jesus Christ—humbled himself to embrace!

Whose power is stronger?
Whose generosity greater?
Who looks more beautiful?
Who loves more tenderly?
Whose manners are more gracious?

If so mighty and excellent a Lord, then, came into the
Virgin's womb and chose to appear scorned, needy, and poor in
this world so that anyone utterly poor and in absolute need of
heavenly nourishment might become rich in Him, then you
should rejoice. Smile! Be joyful!

—Clare of Assisi, *Letters*—

I looked up at the bright sky and heard different kinds of
music in it:
O glorious living light, living in holiness!
O angels who—in the middle of the mystical darkness
surrounding all creatures—look eagerly on God!
How joyful it must be to be an angel,
and be free from every kind of evil.

O angels with shining faces who guard the people.
O archangels, who take honest souls to heaven.
O virtues and powers and principalities and
dominions and thrones.
O cherubim and seraphim.

Praise be to you all, seeing the heart of the Father,
looking on the Ancient of Days gushing up in the fountain,
praising His inner power
appearing like a kind face.

—Hildegard of Bingen, *Scivias*—

january 8 ✿

Sweet eternal will of God, you've taught us how to find you. If we asked our kind, loving Savior and most merciful Father, "How can we find You?" God would tell us: "If you want to find and experience the fruit of My will, always live in the cell of your soul." Now the cell is a well of both earth and water. We can understand the earth to be our own poverty when we recognize that of ourselves we're nothing. That's why we must admit our being comes to us from God. He is living water.

Let us plunge into this well!

—Catherine of Siena, *Letters*—

january 9 ✿

Wise Love,
you keep holy order
as you praise God and know God in your praising.
You accomplish God's will in all things
when you do this.

And if we praise God faithfully,
we'll rest in God, and
this will be the cause of our rejoicing.

—Mechthild of Magdeburg—
The Flowing Light of the Godhead

january 10 🌿

Sweet measureless love, who moved you? Love alone. O gentlest love, Jesus! To strengthen each person's soul and free it from the weaknesses it fell into knowing through disobedience, You built a wall around it, mixing the flow of Your own blood into the lime for the mortar. This blood fuses the soul with God's gentle, divine will and fits it for His love because just as lime mixed with water is put between stone and stone to bind them together securely, so God mixed the blood of His only-begotten Son into the living lime, the fire of God's shining love.

God put this celestial cement between Himself and every one of His creatures—because there is no blood without fire, nor fire without blood.

—Catherine of Siena, *Letters*—

THE SOUL (burdened and bad-tempered): I hate long working hours! I'm weary of the tiring load I carry while on earth! I find it hard to fight my humanness.

VIRTUES: Dear Soul, God's will created you, you happy catalyst of good! Why be weak against the thing God crushed with the Virgin's help? Through us you can conquer the devil.

THE SOUL: Help! Give me strength. Help me stand firm.

KNOWLEDGE OF GOD: Remember the grace you wear, daughter of salvation, and stand strong. Then you'll never fail.

THE SOUL: But I don't know what to do or where to run. I am afraid. I'm not able to wear my clothing well. I want to tear it off.

VIRTUES: Miserable soul, why do you hide your face from your Creator?

KNOWLEDGE OF GOD: Why do you refuse to see or taste the One who made you?

HUMILTY: I, Humility, queen of the virtues, have something to say: Come to me, every virtue. I'll strengthen you. Then you can seek the lost coin and give it the crown of joyful perseverance.

VIRTUES: Glorious queen, kindest mediator, we come, dancing!

THE SOUL (in the body, repentant and lamenting): Divine virtues, you shine so marvelously in the highest Sun, and your home is so sweet!

—Hildegard of Bingen, *Scivias*—

january 12 🌿

Praises must always be offered to the divine Creator. Praise God with your heart and mouth, for by His grace He sets on heavenly thrones not only those who stand erect, but also those who bend and fall.

—Hildegard of Bingen, *Scivias*—

The Way God Approaches the Soul:
I come to my beloved as the dew on the flower.

—Mechthild of Magdeburg—
The Flowing Light of the Godhead

january 13 🌿

If you want to understand what's in my book, *The Mirror of Simple Souls*, be careful what you say about it because it's very hard to comprehend. First, you must be overwhelmed by Humility. She's the keeper of Wisdom's coffers and the mother of every other virtue. Even you brilliant theologians and you smart students won't have any intellect for *The Mirror*—no matter if you're geniuses—if you don't read my book humbly. Only then can Love and Faith, the ladies of the house, help you rise above Reason.

Reason boldly admits that she doesn't live apart from Love and Faith. Reason says they act as her lord, and she must humble herself before them. So humble your wisdom that's based on

Reason. Place your trust in everything Love gives you, as shown through Faith. That's how you'll understand this book that makes the Soul live by loving.

—Marguerite Porete, *The Mirror of Simple Souls*—

january 14 🌿

God be with you. God will teach you the true ways of agape Love. Your part is to be vigilant and discerning in all you do.

Consider your journey. Remember who you are. Be firm in your faith.

If you earnestly desire eternal life and do not follow your emotions but God's will, you will possess everything His love desires for you. So live in joyful hope. Be utterly confident that God will allow you to love Him with that great love with which He loves Himself.

—Hadewijch, *Letters*—

january 15 🌿

The Soul Praises God for Five Things:
You're the Emperor of praise!
You're the Crown of every king and queen!
You're the Wisdom of the most learned!

You're the Giver of every gift!
You're the Deliverer from each addiction!

—Mechthild of Magdeburg—
The Flowing Light of the Godhead

january 16 ❦

Prayer unites the soul to God. Although the soul is like God in nature, it is often different from Him in condition because of a person's sin. Prayer then acts as a witness that the soul wills as God wills. It eases the conscience and prepares us for grace. That's why God teaches us to pray—to trust without doubting that we will have grace, for the Lord looks on us in love. God wants nothing more than to make us partners in His good will and work.

—Julian of Norwich, *Revelations*—

january 17 ❦

Sin is unclean and unnatural—and horrible. However, the loving soul wanting to be beautiful and shining in God's sight shouldn't be afraid of sin, except to the point that fear is useful. Instead, we should humble ourselves and weep over our weaknesses to God, our beloved Mother, who'll sprinkle us with

His precious blood, and our souls will become as supple and as kind as possible.

God always heals us, and with the most amazing gentleness over time. It does take time for us to heal in ways that will bring God the most glory, and us the most joy, forever. The Lord never stops or even slows His kind, gentling healing in us.

—Julian of Norwich, *Revelations*—

january 18 🌿

O tall mountains
of confidence in God,
you never surrender when the Lord tests you!
Although you stand far away from me
as if in exile, all alone,
you remind me that
no armed power is strong enough to best you.

Your trust in God is wonderful!

—Hildegard of Bingen, *Book of Divine Works*—

january 19 🌿

When we trust in God, we live in the light of true faith, and our obedient souls are set on fire in the furnace of divine love. We're anointed then with humility and become inebriated in Christ's blood. Then the sister of Humility—Patience—and the submissiveness she teaches us helps us accept umpteen spiritual rewards from God, our Creator and Friend. We become courageous then and persevering, and we are also able to enjoy all the other virtues God gives, as well as their fruits.

—Catherine of Siena, *Dialogue*—

january 20 🌿

Miserable sin, what are you? You're nothing. I looked and saw God is in everything. And I didn't see you then. When I saw God made everything, I didn't see you. When I saw God is in everything, I didn't see you. When I saw God does everything that's done—both great and small—I didn't see you, either.

When I saw our Lord Jesus Christ seated in our soul so well—I saw love and delight, good laws and protection, and all that He has made there—but I didn't see you. That's why, sin, I'm certain you're nothing.

—Julian of Norwich, *Revelations*—

january 21 🌿

Be happy. Be content—always, everywhere, in all circumstances—because every circumstance is a gift of love for you from the Eternal Father. That's why God wants us to rejoice in every one of our troubles, and to praise and give glory to His name—yes, in everything—because God loves you with a forever kind of love.

Buck up! Remember who loves you, and be encouraged today and every day in Christ, gentle Jesus.

—Catherine of Siena, *Letters*—

january 22 🌿

We praise You, Lord, that You searched for us in Your humility.
We praise You, Lord, that You kept us in Your mercy.
We praise You, Lord, that You adored us in Your humiliation.
We praise You, Lord, that You provided for us in Your generosity.
We praise You, Lord, that You watched over us with Your strength.
We praise You, Lord, that You made us good with Your goodness.
We praise You, Lord, that You taught us in Your intimacy.
We praise You, Lord, that You lifted us up in Your love.

—Mechthild of Magdeburg—
The Flowing Light of the Godhead

You're the highest, infinite God. You're good above every good. You're joyous good. You're good beyond measure and understanding. You're beauty above every other sort of beauty. You're wisdom above all wisdom. You're wisdom itself and the food of angels, and You are given to us with a burning love.

You're the clothes that cover all nakedness. You pasture the starving within Your sweetness. How sweet You are, God, with no hint of bitterness!

—Catherine of Siena, *Dialogue*—

God Compares the Soul to Four Things:
You taste sweet as grapes.
Your fragrance is as intoxicating as balsam.
Your radiance is like the brightness of the sun.
And you're the maturity of my most sublime love.

The soul always follows a rare and excellent path, and she draws the senses after her in joyful obedience.

—Mechthild of Magdeburg—
The Flowing Light of the Godhead

The Lord only promises the kingdom of heaven to the poor. That's because anyone who loves temporary material blessings loses the fruits of love. No one can serve both God and money because either one will be loved and the other hated, or one will be served and the other detested.

You also know this is true: A person wearing clothes is at a disadvantage in a fight with a person who's naked because the person in clothes is more easily thrown. Clothes give the opponent a place to make purchase on this person. Just so, anyone who revels in the glories of earth can't rule with Christ in heaven. Jesus did say, "It's easier for a camel to pass through the eye of a needle than for a rich person to enter the kingdom of heaven."

So give away your clothes—your earthly possessions and riches—and you won't be pinned by the one fighting against you. Then you can enter the kingdom of heaven via the straight path and the narrow gate. What a great swap! To exchange the things of time for the things of eternity, to select heavenly gold over earthly goods, to get one hundred gifts instead of one, to enjoy life everlasting.

—Clare of Assisi, *Letters*—

I'm not good because of any revelations I've had. No. I'm good only if I love God better. Also, however much you love God more than I do, you're closer to God than I am.

I don't say this to the wise. You already know it. I say it to those of you who admire my revelations. Be comforted and strengthened, because we're all one in love. God certainly didn't reveal to me that He loves me better than the humblest soul who's in a state of grace. I'm sure there are many who've never had revelations or visions—only the usual teaching of the Holy Church—who love God better than I do.

If I pay special attention to myself, I'm nothing, but in general I am—I hope—unified with my fellow Christians in love. This union holds salvation because God is everything that is good, God made everything that is made, and God loves everything that He made. The person who loves everything and everyone God made, loves God because God is in every person. God is in all things.

The person who loves everything loves as God loves.

—Julian of Norwich, *Revelations*—

I was twenty-six when—on January 27—I was in church and looked up and saw a handsome young man about sixteen years old standing in front of me. I was young then, and found his good looks very appealing.

He told me in a polite, gentle voice, "You'll soon be saved. Why are you so sad? Is it because you've got nobody to talk to, nobody to tell how unhappy you feel?" Then he added, "Don't worry. I'm going to save you. I'm going to deliver you. Now don't be afraid."

When he said this, I saw he was holding my hand as if he was pledging his heart to me. His hand was as handsome as the rest of him.

He said, "Consorting with my enemies, you've licked dust and sucked honey among the thorns. Come back to me, won't you. I'll make you drunk with my divine pleasure."

That's when I saw that between him and me was a hedge so long I couldn't see either end of it. At the top, it bristled with thorns. They were so huge I realized it was impossible for me to get over this horrible hedge to the young man. I hesitated. I was burning with desire. I felt faint, when suddenly he grabbed me and lifted me up effortlessly and put me down beside him.

On the hand of his that I'd held, and that had pledged eternal love to me, I saw those shiny jewels—his wounds—that had canceled all my debts. That's why I praise and adore and thank You as best I can for Your wise kindness and kind wisdom. You, my Creator and Savior, wanted to gentle my stiff-necked stubbornness under Your happy yoke.

21

From then on, I knew a new spirit of joy and tranquility. I followed the path of Your fragrance from then on. I found Your sweet yoke and Your light burden when, ironically, just a short time before that encounter I'd found them both absolutely unbearable.

—Gertrude the Great, *The Herald of Divine Love*

january 28 🌿

With the well-tuned, harmonious harp of Your divine heart,
and through the power of Your Holy Spirit, the Paraclete,
I sing to You, Lord God, lovable Father.
I sing You songs of praise and thanksgiving for all creatures
in heaven, on earth, and under the earth,
for all which are and were and will be born.

I give You thanks to the best of my ability, Lord God.
You created and re-create me.
Thank You for Your kind forgiveness
and for reassuring me of Your unending love,
flowing down from up above.

Be my honor, Lord,
my joy,
my beauty,
my consolation in sorrow,

my counsel in uncertainty,
my defense in everything unfair,
my patience in problems,
my abundance in poverty,
my food in fasting,
my sleep in vigilance,
and my therapy in weakness.

—Gertrude the Great—
Hymn of Thanksgiving; Spiritual Exercises

january 29 🌿

As another new year begins for us,
we're already looking forward to spring's
green mountains and fields and blooming flowers.
We're already looking forward to that beautiful time,
even though the landscape is still winter-brown.

That's exactly how it is for anyone who gives
their all for Love's good-looking promises,
before measuring Love's immeasurableness.

Their joy isn't ripe yet,
but it will be.

—Hadewijch, *Poems in Stanzas*—

january 30 🔥

Don't forget to scrutinize your heart at all times, and with joy. Study what you yearn for and look with the holy truth of God's Spirit into the innermost desires of your heart.

If you do this on a regular basis, you'll find all lying repugnant. You won't want to lie anymore because you'll realize that lying drives God's love out. Lying damages your soul, and you won't want that. Lying strengthens secret cunning, hate, and rage in your heart. Don't let it take root.

—Mechthild of Magdeburg—
The Flowing Light of the Godhead

january 31 🔥

The Lord reminded me one day, "You're My own true wife. Remember that I loved you so much that I died for you? Don't forget that. Remember, too, that a wife takes pleasure in being at her husband's side. A wife loves her husband and enjoys his company immensely—above all others'—because that's where she finds true acceptance, her greatest joy, and also her greatest peace."

—Margery Kempe, *The Book of Margery Kempe*—

february

february 1 🌱

I wish Love would give me new days
because these I have right now are very old.
If that could be,
then I'd stop complaining
about so many things
and live carefree, fully trusting in Love,
but instead I now seem to meet with frightening risks
on every side.

Still, never mind. No matter how joyful I'd be then,
I choose to grant Love the right to do with me
as Love sees fit, according to her pleasure.

—Hadewijch, *Poems in Stanzas*—

27

february 2 🌿

Indescribable, blazing love! Sweet love! Open our memory up for us, so we can receive, remember, and grasp the great goodness of God. As much as we understand God's goodness, we'll love, and whenever we love, we find ourselves in union with and transformed by that love. The mother of all virtues is love.

This love passed through and is always passing through the gate that is Christ crucified.

—Catherine of Siena, *Letters*—

february 3 🌿

Dear hearts! Don't let your heavy griefs get you down!
You'll blossom soon, I promise you.
You'll ride out hard times and make it through all storms.
You'll arrive at last at that verdant land
where Beloved and loved-one totally flow into each other.

To that end, stay faithful here on earth.

—Hadewijch, *Poems in Stanzas*—

february 4 🌿

May you be so strong and filled to overflowing with the Holy Spirit who came upon the holy disciples that God's gentle word can grow and bear fruit in you and in your neighbors, too.

After the fire of the Holy Spirit descended on the disciples, they mounted the pulpit of the blazing Cross, where they felt and tasted the hunger of God's Son, and Christ's hunger was God's love for all people all over the world.

Make your home in the pulpit of the cross. Be engulfed there. Lose yourself completely, with unsatisfiable desire for God.

—Catherine of Siena, *Letters*—

february 5 🌿

I saw so many fiery devils opening their mouths, I thought they'd swallow me alive. There were so many of them, I lost track, I can't say how many devils I saw in how many days. They frightened me every waking moment.

They said I must abandon the church, my faith, God, Mary, and every saint in heaven. They shouted at me and told me to deny my good works and any small virtue I had. They told me to abandon my father, mother, friends, and husband, and so I did. They abused me with their words.

I said many cruel things to them and felt I had no goodness in me. I wanted to be mean to them. The evil spirits tempted me, and I followed them. Many times I wanted to kill myself. I wanted to be damned in hell with them. To prove it, I bit my hand so badly that to this day I have the scar. I also tore my hair and scratched my skin. I hit my breast with my fists and scratched around my heart with my nails. I would've done more, but I was restrained both day and night. I suffered these troubles for a long time. Many people thought I'd never recover or live to see another day, even.

But then, I was lying by myself one day, with no one tending to me, when our merciful Lord Jesus Christ—Who is so reliable, blessed be His name—appeared to me, even though I'd forsaken Him. He was the most wonderful-looking Person I'd ever seen. He wore a purple silk cloak when He sat on my bed and looked at me, and His eyes were so joyful my soul felt strengthened suddenly. I felt peace.

Then He asked, "My daughter, why did you leave Me, when I never for one moment left you, remember?" Immediately, the whole room became bright as lightning, and He rose unhurriedly into the air. I watched him go, until I could no longer see Him. At once, I became calm again. I came to my senses then.

—Margery Kempe, *The Book of Margery Kempe*—

february 6 ❦

Sweet Jesus, I've chosen You above all others. You're the most trustworthy Lover of my soul and the best partner of my life. My rational soul pines for You. I offer my heart to You. I choose You as my companion and guide. I offer You myself—body and soul—as Your servant. I belong to You, and You belong to me.

Cement me to You, my true Love. Your love, kindness, and gentleness attract me to You. When I obey You, I tie myself to You, and clinging to You is the best love anyone can experience. Loving You is the sweetest thing I know. It's what I want more than anything else.

Christ says, "I'll support you in my Holy Spirit. I'll draw you close to me in inseparable union. You'll be my guest. I'll hug you to my happy, cherishing love. I'll make you a robe of the finest purple of my precious blood. I'll fill up your desire with Myself, and that's how I'll make you glad forever."

—Gertrude the Great, *Spiritual Exercises*—

february 7 ❦

In the Psalms God encourages us to delight ourselves in the Lord and He will give us the desires of our hearts. Put your delight in the Trinity. The Lord says to us today, "Put your heart's delight nowhere else but right here in My divine heart, and lay your head down joyfully on My human chest, because I am the only place that will ever bring you real comfort. Rest here in the unique kisses that My Spirit wants to give you."

—Mechthild of Magdeburg—
The Flowing Light of the Godhead

february 8 🌱

If you need love, God's the love you need because the power of His love kept Him nailed fast to the cross. Only the power of love kept the God-Man bound there, not mere cross and nails.

I'm not surprised that those who make their souls a garden of self-knowledge are strong in the face of the world's confusion. They're fitted to and made one with supreme strength. In this life they truly begin to taste eternal life. They control the world by making light of it. The devils are afraid to get near a soul on fire with divine love.

—Catherine of Siena, *Letters*—

february 9 🌱

SOUL: Lord, You're constantly lovesick for me,
and You came to earth and showed me that in person.
You've written me into Your book of the Godhead.

You've embraced me in Your humanity.
You've buried me in Your side, in Your hands and feet.
Allow me, Beloved, to pour balsam on your love-sick
wounds.

GOD: O, sweetheart, but where will you get the balm?

SOUL: Well, Lord, I was going to tear the heart of my soul in
two. Then I thought I'd put You in it.

GOD: Ah, now. You could never give me a more soothing
balsam than that of letting me lie in your soul forever,
weightlessly.

SOUL: Then take me home with You, Lord. Let me come with
You. I'm happy to be Your physician forever.

—Mechthild of Magdeburg—
The Flowing Light of the Godhead

february 10 🌿

God says, "Everyone who's willing to carry the key of obedience gains life through the gentle Christ Jesus. I, God, made My
Son a bridge for you because the road to heaven had been
destroyed.

"If you walk along this pleasant, straight path, well-lighted
by truth, holding the key of obedience, you'll make it through
the darkness of this world without stumbling. In the end, you'll
unlock heaven with the key of my Word."

—Catherine of Siena, *Dialogue*—

february 11 🌿

When you see your neighbor having any kind of trouble, those of you who are spiritual should never become stuck on your own good fortune and presume to judge or look down on your neighbor then. When enlightened by the light of humility, the soul sees itself with keen eyes and becomes aware of the fact that it's been in the same dilemma as its neighbor, or—if it hasn't been in that exact same predicament—it knows it wasn't able to stand alone and resist falling, but that God's grace stood by it and helped it.

The spiritual person doesn't judge her own neighbor and feel pride. Instead, when the spiritual person sees her neighbor having problems, it's a reason for being more humble.

—Angela of Foligno, *Instructions*—

february 12 🌿

Although physically small, people are powerful in their souls. The head of the soul looks up, and its feet are on solid ground. It can put into motion both exalted and common things. Whatever it does echoes through the universe because its inner humanity has the power to accomplish such kind things.

A person's body is bigger than a person's physical heart, just as the soul is more powerful than the body. A person's heart lies hidden within the body, just as the body is surrounded by the powers of the soul, because these cover the entire globe. That's why you exist in the knowledge of God and are able to do your best for God spiritually and also in worldly matters. Remember, whether you have success in what you do or failure, always focus on God. Constantly praise Him and respect Him.

With your physical eyes you can see all the creatures on this earth. With the eyes of faith you should always look at the Lord in confidence. It's God that we see in every creature, because we know He's the Creator of the whole world.

—Hildegard of Bingen, *Book of Divine Works*—

february 13 🌿

I know you're going to ask me, since I talk so much about agape love, "But what if I have no such unconditional love in me and no great tenderness (and I don't), and yet you say without such love I'm powerless; so then, how can I get it?"

I'll tell you how. Love is only had by loving. So be up and doing. And remember that there's nothing so difficult and no stronghold so impregnable that it can't be broken down (and you built up) by Love.

—Catherine of Siena, *Letters*—

february 14

Would you like to know your Lord's meaning?

Okay, then know it well. The Lord's meaning is love. Love is his only meaning.

Who shows this to you? Love.

What did He show you? Love.

And why does He show it to you? For love.

Stay in God's love, then, and you'll learn more about its unconditional, unending, joyful nature. And you'll see for yourself, all manner of things will be well.

—Julian of Norwich, *Revelations*—

february 15

Pick up the key of obedience. Go on, pick it up. What are you waiting for, really? Why not take it right now? You can do that if you're living by the light of a confident trusting in God. You don't have to walk in blindness and bitter cold today. All you have to do is cling instead to obedience with a burning love that God will give you. It will make you warm, and its warmth is the best heat.

God says, "Follow my kind, true Law, and there's no doubt then you'll taste eternal life."

Go on, try it.

—Catherine of Siena, *Dialogue*—

february 16 🌢

Our lives can be analyzed into three divine parts. The first part is our essence, the second our growth, and the third our completion. Essence belongs to God's very own nature. Growth belongs to mercy. Completion belongs to grace.

These three parts correspond to the Trinity's three Persons, as God showed me. The divine, creative power of the Trinity is our Father. The mysterious wisdom of the Trinity is our Mother. And the wonderful love of the Trinity is our Lord, the Holy Spirit.

We were born with these correspondences. But then I saw more. I saw that when Jesus—who as the second person of the Trinity is the mother of our spiritual growth—came to earth, Christ become the mother of our senses, too, because we are made of things both invisible and not.

—Julian of Norwich, *Revelations*—

february 17 🌢

I'm like a fish resting in the ocean. The waves rush over the little fish, and the great storms buffet; but this fish goes on swimming, knowing capture is impossible, and the storms just make this fish leap with more agility.

That's what I do in this world that is a troubled sea. The great currents arrive, and I sail below them. I take shelter in You, God, and let them pass by. Then my soul finds wings in the two arms of Christ on the cross, and I rush up, Jesus, into Your protection and saving grace.

When I stop and remember that I'm with You, I don't fear the currents. I conquer them by navigating through them in Your peace, and I come out of all storms unharmed. But without You, I'd be just like a whale stuck on the beach at high tide, condemned to death.

—Umiltà of Faenza, *Sermons*—

february 18 ❧

God reminded me, "Although the bridge of grace is raised up high, it remains connected to the earth. Do you know when it was raised up? When My Son was nailed on the wood of that most holy cross, He didn't separate His exalted, divine nature from the lowly earth of your humanity. Christ was raised up high on the cross then, but He remained on the earth.

"In fact, the Lord's divinity is kneaded into the clay of your humanity. They make one bread. No one could walk on that bridge until My Son was raised up high on the cross. That's why Jesus said that when He is lifted up high, He will draw everything to Himself, as St. John records in his Gospel. What Jesus said is true because everything was created for you to use, to serve your needs; however, you who have the gift of reason weren't made for yourselves, but for Me, to serve Me with all your heart and all your love.

"So when you're drawn to Me, everything's drawn with you because everything was made for you. That's why it was necessary for this bridge to be raised up high, and that's why it had to have stairs—so you'd be able to climb it more easily.

"To keep out rain and mud and make it easier for travelers to walk along it, this bridge has a roof of mercy and walls of stone made of true, solid virtue, hewn from the body of my Word (and My gentle Son tempered the mortar with His own blood). At the end of this bridge is the entrance. That's why Jesus said that He is the way, the truth, and the life. Whoever walks with Him doesn't walk in darkness but in the light, as St. John wrote in his Gospel."

—Catherine of Siena, *Dialogue*—

february 19 🌿

Love alone is the only thing that can satisfy us. Nothing else can. And you know that. Love always rewards the one who loves, but I will admit that sometimes Love seems to come all too slowly, at its own snail's pace. You can't hurry it, though, so don't ever let yourself give up on God and His love. Remember that Love may come slowly, but you can be sure Love will always arrive right on time. So wait on Love. And God be with you.

—Hadewijch, *Letters*—

february 20 🌿

The Eternal Truth says, "My infinite good can't be contained by anything less than itself, just like a ship at sea can't ever hold the whole sea. The ship can only hold as much as it can hold, and no more. Only the ocean contains itself fully.

"In the same way, I who am the sea of Peace am the only one who can contain and appreciate Myself fully. This makes Me rejoice in Myself, and of course I share all My joy and all My good with you, with each of you, as you are able to accept them.

"May you know and embrace as much of My goodness as I give you."

—Catherine of Siena, *Dialogue*—

february 21 🌿

Everything I've said is nothing
when you compare it to what I've felt within—
the joyful dance of love
between God and the Soul,
for when God sees the Soul as pure as it was in the very beginning,
God tugs at it with a glance. God draws the Soul to Himself
and binds it there with a burning love
that on its own would destroy the immortal Soul,
and this is how God transforms the Soul in Him
to know nothing other than God.

Day by day God draws the Soul up into His burning love
until Love has restored it to that pure state it experienced at
the very first.

The Soul being drawn upwards
feels itself melting
in the fire of that sweet Love,
for God will not stop
until He's made the Soul perfect in loving kindness.

—Catherine of Genoa, *Purgation and Purgatory*—

february 22 🌿

Let nothing bother you.
Let nothing scare you.
Everything changes,
always.
Only God is steady and changeless.

But patience hits the target.
Only patience always gets what it wants.
The person who possesses God possesses everything.
That person lacks nothing.
Only God satisfies your every need.

—Teresa of Avila, *Prayers*—

february 23 🌿

Eternal Truth says, "Anger is usually pride made known, but a proud, angry person can't harm someone who's humble because the humble person smothers pride. If you're faithful to Me, your faith can't be lessened by the unfaithfulness of those who want to do evil to you, nor can these same people lessen your hope once you've created it through love of Me. Your hope will be strengthened then, and your love will be proven in your affectionate kindnesses towards your neighbors."

—Catherine of Siena, *Dialogue*—

february 24 🌿

Gentle Truth told me, "When you return good for evil, you prove your own goodness. You, God, also light coals on fire with the love that eventually melts hatred and bitterness from the hearts and minds of those who are full of anger. It will even turn their hatred into tenderness. God's love and great patience are so amazing that His power applauds your persistence and gives you strength when you take up the burden of the sins of those who hate. It helps you bear with their rage and respond in the wisdom of God's love."

—Catherine of Siena, *Dialogue*—

february 25 ❧

Before too long, the sap will flow up
from the roots,
and through its vitality—
near and far—
fields, plants, and trees
will put on their new leaves.

And this is how the world foreshadows this miracle:
The happy birds are chirping,
and the person who becomes a warrior for love
will be conquering soon,
if they are not halfhearted.

— Hadewijch, *Poems in Stanzas*—

february 26 ❧

On the first Sunday during Lent, I saw a bright wheel spinning round and round up in the sky, unbelievably fast. At the top of the wheel I saw a small white bird having the hardest time staying on top of the speedy wheel. Several times it seemed to slip down from the top. Then it struggled back up again to reach the top. It kept at this for some time, slipping down, rising again.

Then I saw a tall, beautiful mountain, and the wheel moved to rest above it. It kept turning, with the little bird clinging to it and persevering. When I came to myself and the trance was over, I thought about that gospel verse that tells us that the way that leads to life is narrow and hard. What indeed is this world if not a wheel going round and round?

Look at everything worldly. You won't find anything not subject to change, and change—by its turning—rolls its subjects from one state to another. One day, you're promoted, and the next, you're pink-slipped. In this state of changeableness, people who follow God and people who don't follow God walk the same wheel, but in different ways.

The good rise as long as they don't pursue temporal pleasures greedily. They're like the white bird of innocence rising on the wheel. Their virtues give them wings, but even they are sometimes driven down by the wheel's power, and yet God's grace always lets them rise to the top again.

But those who grab hold of that wheel meet disaster. Like the bird rising against the wheel, we must use temporal things with the greatest self-control and keep the wings of our virtue flapping in constant motion, always exercising them.

—Elisabeth of Schönau, *Third Book of Visions*—

february 27 🌿

Mothers give their children milk to suck, but Jesus is the sweet Mother who feeds us with Himself. His kindness accomplishes this when we eat the holy Eucharist. This priceless food is life itself, and that's why it strengthens us and helps us grow.

This is how Jesus could say that the holy church preaches Me and teaches you about Me. What do we understand from this? Jesus animates the Eucharist and through it heals us and helps us live abundant lives, in all goodness, being kind to each other.

Mothers also lay their children down on their breasts, for rest and succor, but Jesus is the gentlest Mother who takes us by the hand and leads us into God's breast through His own satisfying open side. I saw Jesus look down there at His gashed side and smile and say to me, "Look here and see how I love you."

—Julian of Norwich, *Revelations*—

february 28 🌿

God says, "Change your ways while you have time. Or your suffering will be enormous because you'll see the devil as he really is. The sight of him is more hideous than any human heart can imagine. Remember when I let you see him as he really is, for the briefest of moments? You said then (after you'd come back to your senses) that you'd rather walk along a road of fire until judgment day than see him again. But even with all you've seen, you've no idea how terrible he really is."

—Catherine of Siena, *Dialogue*—

In every favor the Lord granted me, whether vision or revelation, my soul gained a good deal, and from some visions the gain was very great indeed. Here's an example. My vision of Christ left me with an impression of His extraordinary beauty. To this day I still remember how stunning He looked.

From this vision, I received long-lasting benefits. I had a serious problem that got me into much trouble, and this problem was my obsessive mind. If I saw that someone liked me, and if I happened to be attracted to him also, I then became inordinately fond of this person. I began to obsess over him, though I meant God no harm.

I just couldn't stop my mind from wandering to this person constantly. I would so love seeing him and thinking of him and considering all his good qualities. This obsession began to ruin my soul, but once I'd seen my Lord's incomparable beauty in my vision, I could no longer find anyone who seemed handsome to me by comparison. So after that, no one else could occupy my thoughts like God could. Merely by turning my mind's eyes to look on that gorgeous image of the Lord that I now carry in my soul, I became entirely free from this obsession from that time on.

—Teresa of Avila, *Life*—

march

march 1

May my soul bless You, O Lord my Creator! May my soul bless You from my very marrow. I'll shout Your mercies and extravagant, embracing love! Thank You for Your great mercy. Humbly I praise and adore Your amazing excellence and mercy and goodness, Father of Mercies.

Even when I was leading my unproductive, peaceless life, You were thinking thoughts of peace towards me and not of pain. You were lifting me up with Your countless generous gifts, as though I were better than any other mortal, and my life on earth were one of angelic innocence. What am I, my God, love of my heart? I'm not like You. I'm just a tiny drop of Your goodness, while You're an ocean of gentleness.

Love, open on me—for I am very tiny—the viscera of Your love and kindness. Pour on me the cataracts of Your gracious fatherly nurturing. Break over me fountains of unlimited mercy. Absorb me in the depths of Your love. Drown me in the flood of Your living love, like a drop loses itself in the ocean's fullness. Let me die in the tsunami of Your immense compassion, as a little spark of fire fizzles in the stream's surging current. Let the raindrops of Your kind love make me cling to You.

—Gertrude the Great—
Hymn of Thanksgiving; Spiritual Exercises

march 2 🔥

The song of rejoicing softens hard hearts. It makes tears of godly sorrow flow from them. Singing summons the Holy Spirit. Happy praises offered in simplicity and love lead the faithful to complete harmony, where there's no discord.

So let those still living on earth sing and yearn for heavenly gold because divine grace banishes all dark obscurity. It makes things that are dim to the bodily senses become pure and lucid. That's why everyone who trusts God should offer the Lord praises loyally and tirelessly. Sing to God with joyful devotion, and don't stop.

—Hildegard of Bingen, *Scivias*—

march 3 🔥

Lift yourself completely above the traffic of the world. You must try to do this, and then you will succeed because there's no other way that we can be like Christ. Clothe yourself with Christ crucified. Jesus is the wedding outfit that will give you grace here on earth. When you die, Christ will also give you a place with the genuinely joyful at the table of everlasting life. So keep living in God's holy love. Keep up the good work!

—Catherine of Siena, *Letters*—

march 4 ❧

Each of us has a good conscience that supports God by stepping on our lusts and removing everything that's terribly fiery in our souls. The right hand of the Lord accomplishes this so we can know God and carry out our daily work with respect for our Lord.

This right hand also raises me up in my repentance, even though I was formerly sunk in the swamp of sins. This is the hand that—after I've confessed my sins—creates the power of virtue so I become kindled with the love of God with such longing, I can never have too much of it. That's why I won't die in my sins if I turn to God and repent now.

No, I'll live forever through the humility of pure regret I feel towards God.

—Hildegard of Bingen, *Book of Divine Works*—

march 5 ❧

Remember the overflowing blood of God's Son. Christ bathed us in it when He opened His body up and drained Himself with holy fire and blazing love on the wood of the cross. Love held Jesus there fast. As the saints say, neither cross nor nails could have held God, had it not been for the cement of divine love.

That's why you should always be looking on that wood. Let the eye of your understanding rest on the Cross always. Here you'll discover true virtue and fall in love with it.

—Catherine of Siena, *Letters*—

march 6 🌿

One day after I'd washed my hands and was waiting with the sisters to go into the refectory, the amazing brightness of the sun caught my eye. It was noon, and the sun's shining was especially strong. I thought it was the most beautiful sight I'd ever seen, and it made me wonder, "If the Lord who created the sun, the One on whose beauty even the sun and moon gaze and the One who is Himself a consuming fire, if this Lord is really one with my soul in the way He so often reveals Himself to me, why do I ever treat my companions so coldly and so rudely and even so evilly?"

Love, you are my first-blossoming flower, and for your beauty I forsake this world and consider all earthly joy to be like mud on my feet. I'd rather be married to you!

—Gertrude the Great—
The Herald of Divine Love; *Spiritual Exercises*

march 7 🌿

Be glad. Celebrate! Lose your mindless fear, and take courage today. No, don't ever be afraid, no matter what's happened to you before. That's right, don't be afraid, no matter what you may see coming. Take courage because Christ was crucified for you.

—Catherine of Siena, *Letters*—

The Soul says, "Be calm now, because in the end we'll enjoy God's peace, remember? Keep in mind that I want to and will lead you to the greatest joy in this life."

—Catherine of Genoa, *The Spiritual Dialogue*—

march 8 🌿

I'll drink of you
and you'll drink of me,
and we'll taste all the goodness God put into us.
The person who stands firm is happy.
She doesn't let what God has
poured into her
spill.

—Mechthild of Magdeburg—
The Flowing Light of the Godhead

march 9 🌿

Love gives her children milk. Love feeds her children well. We get this milk in the same way a baby sucks milk from its mother's breast. We get our nourishment by sucking milk through Love's nipple. Just so, our soul can have life only through Christ crucified.

Jesus tells us in the Gospel of John that no one can come to the Father except through Him. Also in this Gospel He tells us that He is the way, the truth, and the life, and that whoever walks with Him doesn't walk in darkness, but in the Light. Walk in that Light.

—Catherine of Siena, *Letters*—

march 10 🌿

A Song of the Soul:
Lord, You shine into my soul
like the sun glows on gold,
and when I rest in You,
what rich joy I have.
In fact, You clothe Yourself, God,
with my soul.
You are her most intimate piece of clothing against the skin.

—Mechthild of Magdeburg—
The Flowing Light of the Godhead

God's Singing Response to the Soul:
God as Lover of the Soul says:
"When I shine, you glow.
When I flow, you grow wet.
When you sigh, you draw My divine heart into you.
When you weep and long for Me, I take you in My arms and
embrace you.
"But when you love, we become one.
And when we two are one,
we can never be separated.
Instead, a joyful sort of waiting
binds us."

—Mechthild of Magdeburg—
The Flowing Light of the Godhead

Here are the signs of true love. Above all, the lover's will
submits to the Beloved's. Then this special, particular love works
in three ways. First, if the Beloved is poor, you try to become
poor. If the Beloved is scorned, you become scorned. Next, this
love begins to abandon all other friendships that compete with it.
It leaves father, mother, sister, brother, and friends vying for the
position of the Beloved in its heart.

Last, you can't keep secrets from your Beloved. This trait completes the others. In the mutual revelation of secrets, hearts are opened, and they become more wonderfully bound to each other.

—Angela of Foligno, *Instructions*—

march 13 🌿

Our merciful Lord Jesus Christ permitted this short auto-biography to be written, to bring glory to His name. It describes some of His wonderful works in my life. By mercy, kindness, and love, He motivated the sinful creature I am to return His love. My life was one of much temptation.

I was like a reed bending when the slightest breeze blows and only standing up straight and tall when the wind ceases its blowing. For many years I was unstable and often overcome by life, but I still found myself attracted to Christ, our Savior. In spite of my emotional ups and downs, the Holy Spirit stirred within me and encouraged me to follow the way of love that Christ, our Savior, walked in sorrow, in His own person, before any of us ever did.

—Margery Kempe, *The Book of Margery Kempe*—

march 14 🌾

The birds that winter oppressed are singing today,
joyful now.
That's us!
We thank Love that before too long we—
proud hearts who've felt great pain—
will be joyful, too.
Our confidence in Love assures us this is true.
Love's power is so great
she'll reward us in ways
we can't begin to imagine.

—Hadewijch, *Poems in Stanzas*—

march 15 🌾

If you really want love, you must begin by loving—I mean you must want to love. Once you want it, open the eye of your understanding to see where and how love is to be found. Then you'll find it within your very self. How? When you see your nothingness.

Once you recognize that in and of yourself you don't even exist, you'll begin to recognize and appreciate God as the source of your existence and of every goodness above and beyond that existence, both earthly and spiritual. Everything we have and

57

everything we discover within ourselves is a gift of God's endless goodness and unlimited, matchless love.

—Catherine of Siena, *Letters*—

march 16 🌿

God, in Your fatherly affection, You said I should think of Your love for me like that of a father who delights in hearing friends and acquaintances compliment his large family of children for their elegance and grace. This father has a toddler also, who hasn't yet matured into the elegance and good manners of the others, and the father feels a special compassion for his youngest child. In fact, the father hugs his awkward child more often than he does the others. The father picks up his littlest one and caresses him with more kind words and little gifts than he gives to his other children.

With this story in mind, You also said that if I had humility and really thought I was the youngest of all, a flood of Your honey-sweet divinity would always flow into my soul.

—Gertrude the Great, *The Herald of Divine Love*—

march 17 🔥

Eternal Trinity, when—through the light of most holy faith—I accepted the light You gave me, I came to know Your way of excellence, made smooth for me by Your many wonderful explanations. That's why I'm able to serve You in the light and not in darkness.

Make me a mirror of a good and holy life. Help me stay awake. Don't ever let me turn again to that miserable life I once led in the darkness, through no fault of Your own. I didn't know Your truth then, so I didn't love it. But I do now.

Why didn't I know You then? The cloud of self-centered love darkened the eye of my understanding, but You came with Your light, Eternal Trinity, and banished all the darkness in me!

—Catherine of Siena, *Dialogue*—

To Mary:
Hail to you, O greenest, most fertile branch!
You budded among breezes and winds
in search of the knowledge of everything holy.
When the time was ripe,
your own branch blossomed.

You're marvelous! And I welcome you here.
The sun's heat releases sweat from you
like the balsam's perfume.
In you, the most stunning flower bloomed
and gave off its graceful fragrance.

All of the herbs and roots
dry and thirsty before your arrival
now grow in all the greens of spring.
Let us praise the Most High forever and ever!

—Hildegard of Bingen, *Book of Divine Works*—

march 19 ❦

Let our hearts and souls explode with love! Let them run to serve our good, sweet Jesus, and respect Him. Let them remember how Christ rescued us from prison and from the devil who once had us in his power.

Our Lord became our bail and surety for us. God himself tore up the deed of bond. When? When Jesus became a servant. When God assumed our own humanity. Still, not even that was enough. Christ had to pay the debt incurred on our behalf. Again, when? On the wood of the most holy cross. O sweet, incomparable, immeasurable Love!

—Catherine of Siena, *Letters*—

march 20 ❦

At the same time that I saw the sight of our good Lord's head bleeding, I received a spiritual vision and a new understanding of God's familiar love for us. I saw God is every good thing to us. Whatever comforts us is our Lord.

The Lord is our clothing, who wraps and covers us for love. The Lord embraces and shelters us. The Lord surrounds us with His love. The Lord never leaves us. God is every good thing.

—Julian of Norwich, *Revelations*—

Dear Lord, Jesus Christ! You're one eternal God with the eternal Father. Remember me. I thank You, Lord, for Your visible kindness to me. Through it You touch me every moment. Your kindness warms my bones, my blood, and my very flesh.

I'll try to repay You, Lord, with a thankful heart, because only then do I feel safe from the dangers of pride. Many things on earth are called good that aren't nearly as good as Your kindnesses to me.

—Mechthild of Magdeburg—
The Flowing Light of the Godhead

I want you to be a tree of love, grafted into the Word who is love, Christ crucified—a tree with its roots in deep humility. If you are a tree of love, sweetly rooted, you'll find the fruit of patience and strength at the tips of your branches, and crowned persever-ance nested within you. You'll find peace and quiet and consolation in suffering when you see yourself conformed in that suffering with Christ crucified. And so, by enduring with Christ crucified, you'll come with joy from much war into much peace. Peace! Peace!

Follow the meekness and patience of the spotless Lamb, Christ, gentle Jesus. Remember you are God's representative.

—Catherine of Siena, *Letters*—

march 23 🌿

People who want a real relationship with God must stoop from sorrow and be penitent during their time spent on earth. Those who are pure and who love God in absolute loyalty are much oppressed and suffer much holy sorrow. With their ever-available loving hearts, they bow before God and bend down under all this pain and are lower than all the other creatures on earth. Pride is rare among them.

—Mechthild of Magdeburg—
The Flowing Light of the Godhead

march 24 🌿

One day, I was feeling so depressed about my past mistakes that I wanted to hide myself completely, and this made the Lord bow to me with such graciousness that heaven's entire court seemed to be restraining Him, astonished.

But the Lord told them, "Nothing can stop Me from following My best friend when she so vigorously pulls at My heart with the cords of her humility."

—Gertrude the Great, *The Herald of Divine Love*—

march 25 🍂

When our disobedience is revealed to us, sometimes we get depressed, and sometimes our bad behavior makes us feel like failures. Spiritual regret can be very frightening, and deep shame can make us believe we have nowhere to turn, and no one to talk with. But it's just not true.

Don't forget that Jesus is a kind Mother. God's Son doesn't want us to run away from Him. God would be distressed if we abandoned Him like that.

—Julian of Norwich, *Revelations*—

march 26 🍂

Lord, You're full, and You fill us with Your kindness, too. You're great, and we're small. Tell us, how are we to become like You then?

Lord, I see You've given us many blessings, and that we must pass these on to others. Although we have a small vessel, You still fill it up. A person can pour the contents of a full, small container into an empty, larger container over and over until the large container becomes full from the contents of the small container. The large container is the satisfaction God gets from our kind actions.

Sadly, we are so tiny that a single petite word from God or from the Bible fills us so completely that for the moment we can't take in any more. We should then pour the gift back again into the large container that is God. How can we do this? Through our holy desires, we must pour our small container of God's love over those we know so that they may work on becoming perfect in God's kindness, and remain that way.

Our Lord God wants us to love Him just as He has loved us and loves us still, and always will. If we want to be like Him, we will love just as He does.

—Mechthild of Magdeburg—
The Flowing Light of the Godhead

march 27 🌿

Holy Spirit,
making life alive,
moving in all things,
You are the source of all creation and all beings.

Holy Spirit,
cleansing the world of every impurity,
forgiving guilt,
anointing wounds,
glistening,
You are commendable.

You are Life.

You awaken and reawaken everything that is.

—Hildegard of Bingen, *Book of Divine Works*—

Constant craving in the soul,
constant pain in the body,
constant daily pain,
constant suffering of the five senses,
constant hope in your heart for nobody but Jesus—

Those who have renounced themselves in God
know exactly what I'm talking about.

—Mechthild of Magdeburg—
The Flowing Light of the Godhead

Unless you are drowned in God's blood, you can never possess that little virtue of true humility, which is actually so great in God's sight. What can you do then? Lock yourself in the open side of the Son of God. Lock yourself in that sweet-smelling spice store where even sin becomes fragrant. There the sweet bride lies down on the bed of blood and fire, and the secret of the heart of God's Son is disrobed and laid bare.

—Catherine of Siena, *Letters*—

march 30 🌿

I hope my words will comfort those who need comfort and will lead all to an understanding of the inexpressible mercy of our Savior, Jesus Christ. May His holy name be worshiped and proclaimed forever. In spite of our own emptiness, in our every day here on earth Jesus shows us much kindness, and God's love gives our daily lives dignity. Jesus always teaches and guides us, and the grace He works in each one of us benefits everyone, as long as we are open to God's endless love.

—Margery Kempe, *The Book of Margery Kempe*—

march 31 🌿

Hope so fills us with holy and humble devotion
that the impotence of the heart
rings in song beautifully before God,
and God loves the notes
that sing in the heart.
Whoever sings along with Hope
will share her success
in celestial love.

—Mechthild of Magdeburg—
The Flowing Light of the Godhead

april

april 1

Alleluia! Mary, Light burst
from your untouched
womb like a flower
on the far side
of death. The world-tree
is blossoming. Two
realms are becoming one.
Alleluia!

—Hildegard of Bingen, *Hymn*—

One day not long after Easter I went to the garden before prime and sat down beside the pond. I began thinking what a pleasant place it was. The clear water and streams, the fresh, spring green of the trees, the birds flying here and there so happily, especially the doves, were all lovely to consider. Most of all, I loved the quiet, hidden tranquility of this secluded place.

I asked myself what else I needed to complete my joy there in such an excellent spot, and I realized I needed a friend. I needed someone intimate, sweet, wise, and fun to share my solitude. Then you, God, led me in meditation back to Yourself, the Source of unimaginable joy. You showed me that if by always praising You, I poured back like water the streams of grace I'd received from You; and if, like a tree, I covered myself in the leaves and blooms of good works; and if, like the doves, I spurned earth and soared towards You, then my heart could accommodate You, and every joy would be mine, with nothing lacking. Throughout the day I thought on these images.

—Gertrude the Great, *The Herald of Divine Love*—

april 3 🔥

On Wednesday of Holy Week, I was meditating on the death of the Son of God incarnate. I was trying to empty my soul of everything else so I could be more focused on His Passion. To think on His death was my overriding desire. Suddenly, a divine word announced in my soul, "My love for you is not a hoax." These words cut me deeply because I saw how true they were. I saw His acts of love and everything the Son of God ever did and suffered, and they revealed that His love for me was no "hoax." I saw God had loved me better and more intimately than anyone else ever could or had.

On the other hand, I saw that my love for God was all about playing games. My love wasn't true. It was a hoax. Becoming aware of this was a mortal blow to me.

—Angela of Foligno, *Instructions*—

april 4 🔥

Wait with blazing desire, deep humility, and much eagerness. If you learn to wait, you'll surely receive our King, who comes to us humble and meek, and seated on a donkey. O endless love! You confound human pride. We see You, the King of kings, approaching humbly, seated on a beast, disgracefully rejected. Let those who seek worldly honor and glory think on this and blush for shame.

—Catherine of Siena, *Letters*—

I saw the profuse bleeding of our Lord's head. Great drops of blood fell from beneath the thorny crown like pellets. These balls of blood were a brownish-red and looked like they came from the veins. The blood was very thick and became bright red as it spread.

As the bleeding continued, I saw and understood many things. There was so much blood that it was like drops of water falling from the eaves of a house after a summer rain shower, falling so thick no human brain could count the drops.

What this vision most taught me was that our good Lord—so absolutely to be revered—makes Himself familiar and kind to us. This intimacy made my soul joyful and confident.

—Julian of Norwich, *Revelations*—

Jesus told His disciples that He longed to celebrate the Passover with them before He died. What does this reference from the Gospel of Luke have to say to us? I want to see us together at the table of the spotless Lamb, who is food, table, and also waiter. The fruits on this table are the true solid virtues. No other table bears fruit, but this one does; and its fruit is splendid and life-giving because this table is Life.

A groove has been beveled into this table, and this one channel flows with blood and water mixed with fire; and if you rest your eye on this channel, you can see the secret of God's heart. I mean, the pierced side of His Son.

This blood is a wine on which our soul gets drunk, and the more we drink, the more we want. We're never fully satisfied because Christ's flesh and blood are joined with the infinite God. Those of us who eat at this table and become like the food we eat begin to love as God does. That's why we run enthusiastically to God's table!

—Catherine of Siena, *Letters*—

april 7 🌿

How should we love God in a holy way? We must love all things that the Holy Trinity commands us to love. Remember, God did not create sin. That's why He hates it in us. God loves goodness in us because God is that Goodness. Then how should we come to know Jesus Christ better? We'll know Christ by His works in the Gospels, and we'll know Jesus when we love Him more than we love ourselves.

How are we meant to follow God's teachings? We must follow the teachings that Jesus taught us and that are still taught today. We are meant to love. We are born for it. And as long as we do this, our joy will increase.

—Mechthild of Magdeburg—
The Flowing Light of the Godhead

My soul felt restless, burning with tremendous desire as I began understanding the unutterable, unending love that God—in His amazing goodness—has for me. I realized how tenderly God loves me and how gently He answers my questions and requests. I saw how God gives me hope in the middle of hard times.

And as my soul gained more light and knowledge, a sweet bitterness in it both mellowed and increased. The hope given me by God mellowed the growing intensity of my soul's ecstasy. However, as a fire burns higher when more fuel is fed to it, so my soul's blazing grew so immense that my body wouldn't have been able to contain it, nor would I have been able to survive the intensity of my feelings of love, had I not been encircled by the strength of God, who is Strength itself.

—Catherine of Siena, *Dialogue*—

april 9 🌿

God, take me to Your house as a servant. Accept me at Your table as if I were Your little dog. Give me the crumbs that fall from the hands of the sweet Christ. They'll be potent to nourish me. Dogs eat the scraps falling from the hands of their master, and those are what I beg You, give me.

—Umiltà of Faenza, *Sermons*—

Start being brave about everything. Drive out darkness and spread light. Don't look at your weaknesses. Realize instead that in Christ crucified you can do everything.

—Catherine of Siena, *Letters*—

april 10 🌿

Defend yourself with virtue.
Then don't worry.
The person who stands firm in God
will conquer their every sorrow
of the heart,
in splendid style.

—Mechthild of Magdeburg—
The Flowing Light of the Godhead

april 11 🌿

O Jesus, gentlest love! Unarmed, and nailed fast to the cross, You defeated our enemies! Jesus, it's really true that You are our peace, our tranquility, our serenity of conscience. No bitterness or sadness or poverty can touch the soul in whom You live by grace.

It stands to reason that such a soul will have perfect happiness and a wealth of joy, for God is happiness itself without a trace of sadness or bitterness. Yes, God is wealth itself. God is the only wealth that never loses its value and that's safe from all thievery.

—Catherine of Siena, *Letters*—

april 12 🌿

Joy and eternal praise be to You, Lord Jesus Christ. Your gorgeous forehead never turned away from what was right and true. Blessed be Your forehead! May all creatures praise it. Amen.

Your bright, compassionate eyes look kindly on all who ask You for grace and mercy, in love. Blessed be Your eyes, eyelids, and wonderful eyebrows! May Your lovely, kind vision be praised forever. Amen.

Your sympathetic ears are happy to listen to everyone who speaks humbly. Blessed be Your ears. May they always be filled with good words. Amen.

Your very clean teeth chewed physical food sensibly for the nourishing of Your holy body. May Your teeth be blessed and honored by every creature. Amen.

You never used Your tongue poorly, and You never kept quiet except honestly and helpfully. You always said whatever God wanted You to say. Blessed be Your tongue. Amen.

My Lord Jesus Christ, blessed be Your throat, stomach, and intestines. May all Your sacred internal workings be honored because they fed You well and kept Your precious body functioning efficiently. They nourished Your bodily life for the redemption of souls, and to the angels' joy. Amen.

You, Lord, are our leader because on Your sacred shoulders and neck You carried the weight of the cross before You smashed the gates of hell forever. Blessed be Your neck and shoulders for enduring so much. Amen.

—Birgitta of Sweden, *Prayers*—

april 13 🖌

Love has many errands. Happy Love, I know what your job is and ever has been and ever will be. You bind God and the human soul together.

Love, help me. You've got more power than all the virtues put together. You do help me. And I thank God for this forever. You free me from many heartaches. I no longer have any virtue myself, but—never mind—Love serves me with all his virtues.

I can do nothing good apart from my Lord, who makes empty hearts full. Alleluia!

—Mechthild of Magdeburg—
The Flowing Light of the Godhead

april 14 🌿

Shame on our human pride and on our self-indulgence and on our self-absorbed love! Shame on these things that we have in spite of God's goodness and the infinite gifts of grace that God showers on us—not because we deserve them—but because He loves us.

We're foolish. We seem not to see or feel the heat of a love so fierce that—were we made of stone—it would have shattered us by now. I'm afraid I can only see one explanation. We simply refuse to lift the eye of knowledge to consider the tree of the cross. Here such heat of love, such sweet and persuasive teaching—rich in life-giving fruit—is made known to us.

There, too, we can see Christ's generosity. It literally tore open God's body so that we could bathe in His blood and be baptized in it every day. The Blood of Jesus swallows up every injury. I'm certain that if the soul really sees this, it won't want anything but to receive the fullness of grace and become complete. It will want to totally destroy and drown its own inappropriate appetites.

The soul will want to be on fire with love for God, forgetting itself like a person in love does. People who are in love forget themselves entirely. They have no time for staring at their navels. Instead, they're totally absorbed in the object of their love. Love has the power to make lover and beloved joined in heart and mind. What one loves, the other loves. They're one.

I've also noticed that whenever we love or really want something (whether this is something useful or something merely bringing us joy or pleasure), we don't care what insult, injury, or trouble we must go through to get it. In fact, we're so intent on getting what we want, we hardly even notice how hard we're working to get it.

Now that's Love.

—Catherine of Siena, *Letters*—

april 15 🔥

The person in pain who complains of a heavy load
is either blind in knowledge
or spineless when it comes to enduring.

That's why our Lord said, "Okay, let Me think about this. I see that you don't want to be sick or disrespected, so I wonder what I could use as the foundation of your glory?"

"Lord, when I'm sick or scorned (and my feelings are hurt), how do I glorify You?"

"When you're ill, I expect you to honor, serve, and love only Me still, and make the effort to be cheerful and patient. And when you're sneered at, you have no choice but to love me and wait. Be tolerant."

—Mechthild of Magdeburg—
The Flowing Light of the Godhead

april 16 🌿

What you hold, may you always hold.
What you do, may you always do.
Never abandon it.
With the swiftest, lightest steps
that stir no dust,
and on feet that don't stumble,
may you walk securely into the future
with joy and speed
along the path of wisdom, happy.

May your steps be practical and sure,
as the Spirit of the Lord calls you.

—Clare of Assisi, *Letters*—

april 17 🌢

Lie down in the fire and see and taste the flowing Godhead in your being. Feel the Holy Spirit move in you, compelling you to love God, His fire, and His flowing in many different ways. After all, what good are big words without works of mercy? What good is your love of God when coupled with a hatred for God-made human beings?

You say, "If God were to give me a forgiving heart, I'd be happy to forgive then." Now, listen here: virtues are partly gifts from God and partly our own doing. Whenever God gives us insight, we should act virtuously. That's how we exercise His goodness in us.

—Mechthild of Magdeburg—
The Flowing Light of the Godhead

april 18 🌢

A ray of God's love wounded my heart, and my soul felt a burning love come out from the divine fountain. I received an ecstasy that was beyond intellect, speech, or emotions. After experiencing that pure divine love, I could never stop thinking about it. It also showed me the magnitude of my ingratitude, and I saw myself in my sins.

This made me despair. I hated myself, and my soul cried out, "O Lord, no more world, no more sins!"

I didn't see sins principally as sins, I saw them as offenses against God's goodness and powerful love. That's what made me turn against myself and try my best to translate that divine love into acts of kindness.

Having witnessed several signs of the intensity and purity of God's love, my soul told my body and my self-love: "If you'll free yourself from superfluous things, you'll no longer be uncomfortable and anxious. Then you'll be thankful for everything I've said and done. You'll share my good forever.

"Be at peace, then, because in the end we'll enjoy God's peace. Remember, I always provide for your true needs. Keep in mind that I, your soul, want whatever will make you happiest."

—Catherine of Genoa, *Spiritual Dialogue*—

april 19 ❦

Perhaps we don't know what love is. It wouldn't surprise me at all to learn that this is true, sad but true. Love doesn't exist—as we like to think—in the degree to which we are happy. No, love exists in the strength of our determination to try to please God in everything that we do, each and every day. The important thing is not to think much but to love much. So start doing whatever most stirs you to love.

—Teresa of Avila, *Interior Castle*—

april 20 ❦

God says, "I want to be merciful to the world. Mercy's what I do. In My unlimited mercy and love for everyone, I sent the Word, My only-begotten Son. To make this amazing good news clear to you, I showed Him to you in the image of a bridge stretching from heaven to earth. This bridge is the union of My divine nature with your human one.

"I, the Eternal Father, supreme and everlasting Truth, am telling you that by following the Word, My only-begotten Son, you have life."

—Catherine of Siena, *Dialogue*—

april 21 ❦

Because you love God beyond what is humanly possible, because you respect God dearly with all your soul's strength, because you know God with all your soul's wisdom, and because you have accepted God's kindnesses and have been very thankful to him, I am writing you this letter. The great flood of divine love never ceases. Instead, it flows on and on without stopping.

It flows on and on effortlessly and sweetly and without failing until, finally, our tiny vessel becomes full and spills over. Yes, we will be filled to overflowing with love if we don't block it with our own sheer self-will. If we don't stop grace with our stubbornness, our small vessel will always overflow with God's kindness.

—Mechthild of Magdeburg—
The Flowing Light of the Godhead

april 22 🌿

Who can hide the beginning and the end, who is, was, and will be forever? And what are you, who are a spark among ashes? What did you know when you were nothing? When pride grows in you, it makes you want to be raised even above the stars and even above the other creatures and the angels, who follow God's teaching in everything.

Now pay attention: What did the devil gain when he opposed Me? Remember? Lucifer tried to raise himself above everything, too. Satan admired his great brightness and tried to lift himself above all creatures. A band of countless proud spirits followed him, but My divine Power defeated them.

—Hildegard of Bingen, *Scivias*—

april 23

What greater good can there be than to live in unity with God who is all good? We can't take credit for the majesty of this union, though, because Love's responsible for it.

A servant maid becomes a great lady when the emperor makes her his wife. By her union with him, she becomes an empress then—not by her own merit (because she was only a servant before)—but because of her new husband's dignity as emperor.

Just think! The soul who falls in love with God—she who is a servant and a slave ransomed by the blood of God's Son—gains such dignity that she can no longer be called a "servant," but an "empress," the spouse of the Eternal Emperor.

How well this agrees with the apostle Paul's words of encouragement that to serve God isn't to be a slave but it is to *reign* with Him in kindness.

—Catherine of Siena, *Letters*—

Greetings to you, living God!
You're my first love.
I'm always glad
I can speak to You honestly.

When my enemies chase me down,
I run to Your arms,
where I can complain about my suffering
and You listen and incline Yourself to me.

You know exactly how to strum
the strings of my soul.

—Mechthild of Magdeburg—
The Flowing Light of the Godhead

God, pierced wine barrel, You offer us a wine that intoxicates every loving impulse. You fill our understanding with joy and light. You flood every memory that's trying to find You, and You leave my heart and soul and mind incapable of remembering, understanding, or loving anything other than Yourself, good, sweet Jesus, Blood and Fire, ineffable Love!

—Catherine of Siena, *Letters*—

april 26 🌿

A beggar woman prayed to God with these words:

"Lord, I thank You that Your love has stripped me of earthly riches and clothed and fed me from the resources of others. I thank You for this because every familiar possession that clings to me and causes me pleasure must become completely foreign to me. Lord, thank You for taking my eyesight from me and for serving me with others' eyes. Thank You for taking the use of my hands away from me and for serving me with the hands of others. Thank You for taking from me the power of my heart and for serving me with others' strong hearts.

"On behalf of all those people who help me, I beg You, reward them here on earth with Your divine love. Help them continue to turn to You and serve You with goodness until they die holy deaths."

Everyone who loves God and leaves this world with a pure heart is an arch-beggar.

—Mechthild of Magdeburg—
The Flowing Light of the Godhead

april 27 🌿

Sweet, eternal will of God, you've taught us how to find you. All we have to do is ask our loving young Savior and most merciful Father, "How are we to find you?"

89

God always answers our questions right away, "If you want to find and experience the fruit of My will, always live in the cell of your soul." This cell is our private place. It contains both earth and water.

The earth is our own poverty. We understand that of ourselves we're nothing. That's why we admit our entire being comes from God. There is living water there, too, which is the true knowledge of God's will. That's why we dive deep into this well, where we come to know both ourselves and God's great goodness.

When we see we're nothing, we become humble, and that humility helps us enter the flaming, burning open heart of Jesus. The heart of Jesus is a window that is always open.

—Catherine of Siena, *Letters*—

april 28 🌿

Now listen to how the Holy Trinity praises Itself with Its endless wisdom and Its everlasting truth and Its entire eternity. Listen to this sweetest, most amazing, happiest music: The Trinity sings with full voice, and all the sweet voices of every saint join in.

The Father sings a hymn of praise: "I am white water, a surging stream no one can stop. But, sad to say, a person can block up the heart easily with a foolish thought and so prevent My restless, ever-working Godhead from flowing into their soul."

The Son sings next: "I'm an ever-running richness contained by no one except the tide of eternity always and forever flowing from God, which returns in its fullness in His Son."

The Holy Spirit joins in: "I'm the undefeatable power of truth. This is found in any person who perseveres in God, come what may." Together, the whole Trinity sing: "I'm so amazingly strong in My unity that nobody can ever separate Me or shatter Me throughout eternity."

—Mechthild of Magdeburg—
The Flowing Light of the Godhead

april 29 🌿

Eternal Trinity, fire and bottomless love! Make my fog of physical troubles vanish. You give me a true knowledge of You that makes me want to leave behind the weight of my body and offer my life for the glory and praise of Your name. By the light of understanding, I've tasted and seen Your profound nature, Eternal Trinity, and the beauty of Your creation.

Then, when I contemplated myself in You, I saw that I'm Your image. You've gifted me with power from Yourself, Eternal Father, and my understanding with Your wisdom. This is the same wisdom belonging to Your only-begotten Son. The Holy Spirit, who comes from You and from Your Son, gives me a godly will, and that's why I'm able to love.

—Catherine of Siena, *Dialogue*—

Courage, my friend, when you think on the answer to this question. Ask, "Immeasurable, sweetest Love, what made You die for us?"

"Love. Only Love."

Jesus, sweetest Love, You wanted to make this soul strong and rid it of the weakness sin gave it, so You built a wall around it by mixing mortar and tremendous amounts of Your blood that blends and molds the soul in conformity with Your sweet will and Your sweet Love.

As lime mixed with water is wedged between stones to bind them securely together, You put the blood of Your only-begotten Son between us and Yourself. You made Your Son into mortar with the living lime of a burning love. There's no blood without fire and no fire without blood because that blood was spilled with the burning love of God for all humanity. Thanks to this wall, the soul is so strong that no wind can bring it down.

—Catherine of Siena, *Letters*—

m a y

The beautiful season of flowers is finally here again!
Those with beautiful hearts
who are chosen to bear Love's chains
also know this season of growing
spiritually as their steady trust-in-God
blossoms in their hands
into flowers and fruits of kindness.

They experience the Word of God
through their blooming spiritual trust.
They're always friends with Love, and
that's why they're intimate with Tenderness.

—Hadewijch, *Poems in Stanzas*—

Patience is wearing a white tunic, embroidered in green in all the folds. She clothes herself in the robe of God's work. This robe is made of the whiteness of perpetual light. The folds are embroidered with the sorrows of the person who laments, "When will I finally see the true Light?"

But we endure this waiting happily in our present life because Patience is thinking about what any delay foreshadows. The very adversities and calamities of the faithful adorn our souls with greenness. That we suffer them in patience on behalf of God makes us all the more beautiful.

—Hildegard of Bingen, *Scivias*—

Thank you so much, Eternal Father, for not abandoning me, Your handiwork. Thank You for not turning Your face away from me. Thank You for not making light of my desires. You are Light, and You've seen and forgiven my dark weaknesses. You are Life, and You've never believed me dead.

You, Doctor, have listened to my grave illnesses of soul.

You, Eternal Purity, have seen and forgiven my terrible habits.

You, Infinite Love, overlook that I am finite, and You, Wisdom, haven't held me accountable for my foolishness. For all these and countless other failings of mine, Your wisdom, kindness, mercy, and infinite goodness haven't hated me.

Instead, in Your light You've given me light, Lord. In your wisdom I've come to know the truth. In Your mercy I've found Your love and affection for my neighbors. What made You do this? Certainly it wasn't my virtues. It was always Your Love. Thank you.

—Catherine of Siena, *Dialogue*—

may 4

In heaven the saints will live in their Creator the way fish live in the sea. Every day they'll be able to drink as much as they want, and they'll never get tired anymore, and also the amount of water available to them will never decrease. There will be no want there.

The saints will experience this abundance because they're drinking and eating God's great sweetness. The more they get of it, the more they'll hunger for it, which is not a problem because this sweetness can't shrink, the same way the water in the ocean can't disappear. All rivers come out of the sea and flow back into it—exactly like the beauty and sweetness of the Lord—and although they flow everywhere, they always return to Him. That's why they never grow smaller.

So even if all you ever did was spend your time thinking about God's great goodness, you could never imagine the love behind the good Lord's sending His Son to us on earth.

—Marguerite d'Oingt, *Mirror*—

After I'd received the body of Christ, I saw that my soul was like a tree fastening its roots in the wound at the right side of Jesus. Then in some new and wonderful way I felt a marvelous sap—the goodness of the humanity and divinity of Jesus Christ—transfusing itself through this wound, as through a root, penetrating into all my branches and fruit and leaves. Surging through my soul, then, the goodness of Christ's whole life shone more brightly, like gold shining through crystal.

—Gertrude the Great, *The Herald of Divine Love*—

Be bathed and drowned in the blood of Jesus Christ. It will make you strong enough to bear with true patience any trial or trouble. God's blood gives you perseverance to endure even to the point of death, and humbly, for in that blood the eye of your understanding will be enlightened by what is true.

And the truth is that God wants nothing more than that we be made holy, for Jesus loves us more than it is possible to say. If God hadn't loved us so much, He would never have paid such a bloody price for us.

—Catherine of Siena, *Letters*—

God whispers to the Soul:
My kindness asks you to wait;
My love asks you to labor;
My patience asks you to keep quiet;
My concern asks you to suffer poverty;
My dishonor asks you to bear up;
My sufficiency asks you not to complain;
My victory asks you to always pursue goodness;
My purpose asks you to endure all things.

—Mechthild of Magdeburg—
The Flowing Light of the Godhead

Open your soul up and embrace your neighbor in love and compassion. Now, there's no way we can have such love unless our eyes are turned like the sharp and invincible eagle's eye toward the brightest, holy tree of life.

O Jesus, gentlest love! You have said, "Do you want an incentive to work for My glory and other people's salvation? Do you want the strength to endure every trial with patience? Then look at Me, the Lamb slain for you on the cross. My blood was totally drained from head to foot. I pay no attention to your foolishness, nor does your ingratitude stop Me from working out your salvation. Look at Me and learn, for I am like one crazed and transformed by My hunger for you."

—Catherine of Siena, *Letters*—

may 9 🌿

When we find that—through God's grace and forgiveness—we are living spiritually harmonious lives, then we'll understand that disobedience is without a doubt more horrible than hell, and more painful. Why? Because it goes against the essential grain of our good, God-given nature.

Sin is both dirty and perverted, and that's why it looks downright ugly to the soul that is shining and beautiful in God. But don't be afraid of sin, except to the point that a healthy respect is helpful.

Instead, whenever we transgress, we should go to our gentle Mother and in all humility confess our disobedience, and we will be sprinkled with God's holy blood, making our souls obedient and tranquil. God heals us all in time, and tenderly.

—Julian of Norwich, *Revelations*—

Kind soul, rejoice!
You become God
when you drink with divine patience
many bitter mouthfuls,
though you are entirely free of guilt.
So—no matter what,
rejoice!

—Mechthild of Magdeburg—
The Flowing Light of the Godhead

Think for a moment about how handsome Jesus Christ is. Stop and think on God's good looks and how they go on and on and on. Christ's beauty is so great and so unending that He's able to give every angel and every one of His friends who live with Him in heaven the gift of being as brilliant as the sun.

If we meditate on Christ's eternal splendor and imagine how gorgeous it must be there with Him where there are so many sparkling lights, then we will center our lives and have everlasting peace.

—Marguerite d'Oingt, *Mirror*—

may 12 🌿

I have a marvelous teacher in the Holy Spirit. God's Spirit teaches me very gently what He wants from me. (Other things the Holy Spirit withholds from me.)

God says to me, "Wisdom without grounding in the Holy Spirit will—in the end—turn into a mountain of arrogance. Peace without the friendship of the Holy Spirit soon becomes an empty rush. Humility without My love ends in hypocrisy. Justice without the depth of My unassuming nature becomes the worst sort of hatred.

"A good life without adversity soon results in a person's becoming lazy and unhelpful. Love that does not have humility as its mother and holy awe as its father is orphaned from all goodness."

—Mechthild of Magdeburg—
The Flowing Light of the Godhead

may 13 🌿

You, Eternal Trinity, are the craftsman, and I am Your carefully crafted (*hand*crafted) piece of work. I've come to understand that You're in love with the beauty of what You've made.

Why? Because You made me a new creation in the blood of Your Son, You who are the deepest love. Eternal Godhead! Deep sea of Love! What more could You have given me, God, than this gift of Your very self?

—Catherine of Siena, *Dialogue*—

may 14 🔥

Faithful love praises God constantly.
Longing love causes a pure heart much sweet suffering.
Searching love is intimate.
Knowing love is gregarious.
Passionate love is mixed with sadness.
Silent love knows much effortless pleasure.
How little the body knows what love does in stillness!

Pure love finds rest in God alone
because these two have one will,
and nobody can disturb them.

—Mechthild of Magdeburg—
The Flowing Light of the Godhead

may 15 🔥

Our Lord said to me, "No one can earn My free gifts. Accept them humbly and be thankful. Be patient when I withdraw them. Don't ever give up. Stay confident until you receive them again. Tears of repentance, spiritual alertness, and compassion are My best gifts. They are treasures without equal anywhere on earth.

"And remember—whatever happens—wherever God is found, that's where heaven is. God is in your soul. Angels surround you. They guard you day and night. When you go to church, I go with you. When you sit at supper, I'm at your side. When you go to bed, I get under the covers with you. When you go out of town, I travel with you even then.

"Daughter, remember, no child was ever as attentive and as ready to please his parent as I am ready to listen to and please you. Let Me help you. I'll protect your every step.

"My grace works much like My sun does on earth. You know how sometimes the sun shines brightly and on those days everyone enjoys its warm rays. On other days, however, the sun is hidden behind the clouds, and it isn't seen all day long; but, remember, its brightness and warmth are still there."

—Margery Kempe, *The Book of Margery Kempe*—

may 16 🌿

A Letter to Hildegard of Bingen:

Be joyful with me, my lady and revered daughter of the Eternal King, because the finger of God writes in you and helps you articulate the Word of Life. You're blessed! May all be well with you forever. You're the mouth of the Holy Spirit because your words burn in my heart, and I burst into these words. My lady, Hildegard, how fitting it is that you are named *Hildegard*, because through you God *protects* his church in spiritual conflicts.

Be strong in the Holy Spirit. The Lord and Creator of all says, "I sent My incarnate Word from heaven's heights into the dark valleys of earth so He would illuminate those who walk in shadows and who think they are something when they're really nothing."

—Elisabeth of Schönau, *Third Book of Visions*—

may 17 🌿

The Lord asked me to make His feet my hallway, His hands my workshop, His mouth my living room, His eyes my library for sitting and reading, and His ears my confessional.

Overwhelmed by love, I said, "Lord, how I want my soul to burn with such fire that it would melt and become a liquid so it could be poured—all of it—into You!"

God answered, "Your will is such a fire for you."

Then I understood that God's will gives us the strength we need to accept every benefit resulting from our good desires towards God.

—Gertrude the Great, *The Herald of Divine Love*—

may 18 🌿

However much we love mercy and practice loyalty, we're like the heavenly Father.

However much we endure poverty, humiliation, rejection, and pain here on earth, we're like the true Son of God. However much we love others and live expansive lives—flowing outward with the abundance of our hearts—and to the extent we give our possessions to the poor and spend our lives serving the sick and the shut-ins, we're like the Holy Spirit. However much we are honest and love peace, and however much we live modest, holy, simple lives, we're like the Holy Trinity.

However much we are disciplined, pure, and humble in complete submissiveness—ready to serve in all holiness and rejecting all hard feelings towards others—we're like Mary. However much we are kind, friendly, and pleasant, we're like the angels.

However much we lead a sanctified life in exile and are sensitive and sad in times of trouble, we're like John the Baptist. However much we want God to be praised, and however much we're thankful for what we've been given, and however much we perform God's will on earth, we're like the prophets and the holy fathers, who through great virtues overcame themselves in God.

However much we learn wisdom, and through it improve other people's lives in the best of ways and stand true to God in hardship, we're like the holy apostles. However much we are patient in suffering, and however much we hold onto our trust in God—even in the face of death—we're like the holy martyrs.

—Mechthild of Magdeburg—
The Flowing Light of the Godhead

Mother is such a beautiful word, so full of sweetness and all that's good, that it really can only be used to describe Jesus. Motherhood is the agape love existing between a woman and the baby at her breast. It's wise, good, and smart.

And even though our corporeal birth is small and simple when compared to our invisible spiritual birth and life, we must remember that Jesus is in the middle of even our corporeal birth, and that without His divine touch, we would not have been born to two earthly parents.

Kind earthly mothers are intimately aware of and responsive to their child's every need. A mother protects and nurtures her child. That is what mothers do. A child will change as it grows up, and to accommodate that change and growing independence, a good mother will alter her approach to her child, but not her love.

Mothers also scold their children when they act on some of their less-appropriate desires, because all loving mothers want to root out bad decisions and unhealthy habits and plant good character in their children. Our Lord is kind to us in this same way.

Our Lord is our Mother, who wants us to be secure in God. And we help God parent us when we love Him, and this love we have for God is set in motion by the generosity of the God-Man born a baby, for Christ is always telling us, "Remember you love Me. Remember who you are, and whose."

—Julian of Norwich, *Revelations*—

Truth tells my heart I am loved by Someone who cares for me unconditionally. This gift delights me past the point of thinking. It transforms me, too, and I become one with divine Love, who reminds me that She enters me and lives in me and gives me the strength to do whatever She wants. The divine Lover gives me this spiritual power.

We are engaged, and so I often say I love God; but I lie. I don't love God, though He loves me entirely. He is and I am not, and I need nothing more than whatever it is that He wants. For example, I need His praiseworthiness. God is completion, and His inclusiveness impregnates me. Love's loyalty is the divinest seed.

—Marguerite Porete, *The Mirror of Simple Souls*—

Our Lord put these words into my mind, "You're written in My hands and feet. See? I'll never forget you. I'm happy I suffered these wounds for you. I'll never get angry and leave you. I'll always love you. So don't be afraid. Don't fear, even if the world seems to be against you. They just don't understand you.

"You must know I'd be happy to suffer everything I've suffered—all over again—and just for you. I don't want you separated from Me forever, no. Know this instead. Just as the priest takes a baby to the baptismal font and dips the baby in the holy water to wash away sin, so do I wash you in My priceless blood to erase every one of your sins.

"Remember—though I do sometimes take away your inner feelings of grace and you find you can't pray or weep, don't let yourself be afraid. Never fear. Instead, remember I'm a hidden God within you."

—Margery Kempe, *The Book of Margery Kempe*—

may 22 🕯

Here's what's best for you to do in fourteen unique situations:
When you pray, be humble.
When you confess, be honest.
When you do penance, do it indefatigably.
When you eat, be sensible.
When you sleep, be disciplined.
When you're alone, be faithful.
When you're with others, be discreet.
When someone teaches you good manners, be receptive.
When someone reprimands you for your mistakes, be patient.
When you do something bad, ask forgiveness immediately.
When you're full of self-absorbed pride, fear for the health of your soul.
When you're sad, trust in God completely.

When you're doing manual work, work hard,
because hard work drives off every evil thought.

—Mechthild of Magdeburg—
The Flowing Light of the Godhead

may 23 ❧

Here's what a friendship with our dearest Companion, our holiest God, is like. In it, intimacy is always possible and can't be stopped, except on our side, for God is always open to us. Nothing can come between us and God, our Spouse, and we can be alone with God whenever we want, as long as we want. All we have to do is desire it.

So let us close the door on our worldly calendars and deadlines and live instead in paradise with the God of love. If we desire this closeness that comes from closing the door on the world, we must realize that that door is our hearts. We don't have to be mystics to accomplish this communion. We only need to focus on God with our will. That's all. It's our own choice, and because God loves us, we can do this.

Don't confuse this state with empty silence. I am speaking of a turning inward and a listening.

—Teresa of Avila, *The Way of Perfection*—

may 24 🌢

During one pilgrimage, in Calais, I was met with great kindness from complete strangers, both men and women. For example, one woman invited me to stay in her home. She even gave me a new outfit to wear. That comforted me to no end! Others invited me to come eat and drink with them. Many other people offered kind words. Through them all, the Lord made my heart joyful. He always sent me such wonderful help and support.

I thanked Him with much sobbing and weeping, because wherever I went, I met with the kindness of countless strangers. May God be praised!

—Margery Kempe, *The Book of Margery Kempe*—

may 25 🌢

Eternal Truth said, "If you hate Me, you're harming both your neighbors and yourself (for *you* are your chief neighbor). The harm done is both general and particular. Hate is generally harmful because it's your duty to love your neighbors as you love your own self. You must love them. This is not a choice. You should pray for them and help them in any way, spiritually or physically, whatever they need. If you can do nothing else, you should at least feel good will towards them.

"If you don't love Me, though, you don't love your neighbors, and you won't help those you don't love. Remember that if you hate someone, you hurt yourself the most, because you are robbing your own self of grace. You also hurt the other person because you're depriving him or her of the prayer and kindness you should be offering to Me on their behalf. Every good thing you give your neighbor should come from the affection you bear them *because you love Me*."

—Catherine of Siena, *Dialogue*—

may 26 🌿

I'm the secret Fire in everything, and everything smells like Me.
The living breathe in My sweet perfume,
and they breathe out praise of Me.
They never die
because I am their Life.

I flame out—intense, godly Life—over the shining fields of corn,
I glow in the shimmer of the fire's embers,
I burn in the sun and the moon and the stars.
The secret Life of Me breathes in the wind
and holds all things together soulfully.

This is God's voice.

—Hildegard of Bingen, *Hymn*—

Discovering God is good—the soul loves God for His goodness. Loving God, the soul wants to possess Him. Wanting God, it gives everything it has or can have—even its own self—to possess Him. Possessing God, the soul fully tastes His sweetness. Possessing, experiencing, and tasting God Himself—the supreme and infinite sweetness—the soul enjoys the greatest pleasure.

Then, the soul falls in love with the sweetness of the Beloved, and wants to hold Him. Wanting to hold God, it hugs Him. Hugging God, it binds itself with God and weds itself to God, and finds God bound and wedded to itself in the sweetest kind of love.

Then, the power of love transforms the lover into the Beloved and the Beloved into the lover. This means that—set on fire by divine love—the soul is transformed by the power of love into God the Beloved, whom it loves with such sweetness.

For this transformation to happen, knowledge must come first, of course. Then comes the love transforming the lover into the Beloved. This is how the soul who knows God in truth and loves Him with passion is transformed into the Good it knows and loves with such passion.

—Angela of Foligno, *Instructions*—

Our good Lord, the Holy Spirit—endless life dwelling in our souls—always protects us and gives us peace. Through grace, God's Spirit brings each soul to tranquility and makes it obedient and reconciles it to God. Our good Lord constantly leads us on this path of mercy while we're in this unpredictable life.

In my vision I saw no anger except on humanity's side, and God forgives us that, for anger is nothing else but an irrationality and our antagonism to peace and love. It comes from a lack of power or a lack of wisdom or a lack of goodness, and this lack is not in God. It is on our side, because—through sin and dejection—we have in us an anger and a constant opposition to peace and love.

In God's lovely look of compassion and sympathy, He revealed this truth often because the foundation of mercy is love, and the business of mercy is to protect us in love. This was revealed to me in such a way that I could perceive nothing about the qualities of mercy outside of the fact that it is all love in love.

—Julian of Norwich, *Revelations*—

One day I felt exhausted because I'd worn myself out. I asked the Lord, "What's up with me? What should I do?"

And the Lord answered me, "I'll comfort you just like a mother comforts her child. Haven't you ever watched a mother hugging her child?"

I went silent. I couldn't remember, so the Lord reminded me of the time six months earlier that I'd watched a mother bending down and holding her little child close to her. He pointed out some things I hadn't noticed at the time. The mother often asked her toddler to kiss her, and to do so this child had to work hard to raise himself up on little legs to reach her cheek. The Lord recommended that I, too, work hard and raise myself up through contemplation to enjoy God's sweet love.

God also pointed out that when this toddler spoke, nobody else there could understand what the little child was saying except the mother. In this same way, only God can understand what a person wants and intends to do, and only God judges a person appropriately, while other people only see exteriors.

—Gertrude the Great, *The Herald of Divine Love*—

God wants us to pursue three gifts. The first is to look for God cheerfully, conscientiously, and without laziness, as best we can, through the Lord's grace. That's why you should search for God with a smile, satisfied, without excessive sadness and useless sorrow.

And the second gift is to wait for God loyally—out of love—without complaining or working against the Lord. God wants us to wait and to be as reliable as He is until our very last day on earth (which can never be far away).

Finally, the third thing God wants is for us to trust Him absolutely, out of complete faith in Him. The Lord wants us to know that He'll appear suddenly and joyfully to all who love Him.

God's work is done in secret, yet the Lord wants to be known. God's coming will be very sudden. God also wants to be trusted because He's so friendly and kind. May the Lord be blessed!

—Julian of Norwich, *Revelations*—

When gold gets to the point of being twenty-four carats,
it can't be purified any more.
That's what happens to the soul
in the fire of God's love.
All of its weaknesses are cast out like dross.
Then, stripped of its fragilities, the soul
rests in God, with no characteristics of its own,
since its purification is the stripping away of the lower self in
us.
Then our being is God.

—Catherine of Genoa, *Purgation and Purgatory*—

j u n e

june 1 🌿

Infinite glory to You, my Lord Jesus Christ! For us, You humbly endured the Cross. Your holy hands and feet were stretched out with rope. Your hands and feet were secured with iron nails to the wood of the cross, cruelly. You were called "Traitor!" You were ridiculed in many ways. Unmentionable words were shouted at You, and—all the while—that title of confusion was inscribed above You.

Eternal praise to You, Lord, for each and every hour You suffered such terrible bitterness and agony on the cross for us sinners! The sharpest pains from Your wounds penetrated Your happy soul and brutally ransacked Your most sacred heart, until it cracked. Then you sent Your spirit out happily and bowed Your head humbly, commending Your soul to the hands of God Your Father.

Then, having died in the body, You remained there, cold on the cross. May You be praised, my Lord! By Your precious blood and holiest death, You redeemed our souls and Your mercy leads us back from exile to eternal life.

—Birgitta of Sweden, *Prayers*—

june 2 🌿

Mercy is a compassionate quality. It belongs to motherhood in tender love. Grace is worthy of praise, too, because it is a quality that belongs to God's magnificent power in that same love. Mercy protects, endures, energizes, and heals, and is every tenderness of love. Grace is mercy's helper. It raises, rewards, and always exceeds what our love and labor deserve.

Grace is evidence of God's amazing abundance, and we see through it that this divine generosity emanates from God's kingly authority and wonderful kindnesses. Grace comes from this abundance of love and transforms our horrible mistakes into abundant, unending consolation. Grace alters our shameful falling into a high, honorable rising, and grace transforms our sorrowful dying into holy, joyful living.

—Julian of Norwich, *Revelations*—

june 3 🌿

May the eye of your mind transcend your own self, and may you look with love into the eye of divine compassion because this is exactly how God looked on us, His creatures, before He created us. He still looks on us with this very same love. When He first saw us within Himself, He fell so totally in love with us that— because of this love—He created us to share and enjoy the good He possesses in Himself.

However, Adam's sin stopped His desire from being fully realized. Then the fire of divine love moved God, and He sent the gentle incarnate Word, His Son, to ransom and rescue us from slavery. This same love made His Son run to surrender Himself to the cross and its shame.

See? That's why you can't put laws or limits on love. The spotless Lamb possesses an unspeakably compassionate love, unendingly.

—Catherine of Siena, *Letters*—

june 4 ❧

You called me to You, Lord, even though I didn't deserve it. But Your mercy made our friendship possible. If anyone knew my every sin as You do, they'd be astounded at Your mercy and inexplicable goodness. I wish everyone could thank You for Your kindness to me, but this is just how You operate: You make empty creatures good. Your presence gives the world its worth, and we thank and praise You.

Lord, have mercy on heretics, tax dodgers, thieves, adulterers, prostitutes, and every criminal. Spare them in Your clemency. Help them resist temptation. Strengthen everyone who has an addiction. Help those who suffer endless temptations. Give them the grace to stand firm and endure their weaknesses.

Have mercy on all confessors and preachers and on everyone who represents You here on earth. Pour much grace into their souls. And have mercy on all my children, both those born of my body and those born of my spirit. Have mercy on all my friends and on everyone who doesn't like me. Have mercy on the sick, especially all lepers and those confined to their sick beds. Have mercy on those in prison. Have mercy on everyone who's ever said kind things about me, and be kind to those who've said damaging words about me, too.

Thank You for every bad thing that has come my way and for those still to come as long as I live. I bless my God in my soul.

—Margery Kempe, *The Book of Margery Kempe*—

june 5 🌿

The sweet dew of the Eternal Trinity sprang up out of the fountain of the everlasting Godhead into the flower of the chosen maid, and the fruit of this flower is an immortal God and a mortal Man and a living hope of eternal life. This is how our Redeemer became our Bridegroom. And the bride (the soul) is exhilarated at the sight of his kind face:

The narrower the bed of love becomes, the more intense are the embraces.

The sweeter the kisses on the mouth become, the more lovingly do the lovers stare at
each other.

The greater the sorrow when they part, the more treasures will he give her.

124

And the more she consumes, the more does she possess.
The more humbly that she takes her leave, the sooner will
she return.
The greater her passion, the more quickly does she burst into
flame.
And the more she burns, the more beautifully does she glow.
And, yes, the more God's praise is shared with the world, the
greater her desire.

—Mechthild of Magdeburg—
The Flowing Light of the Godhead

june 6 🌿

God did not make life unfair. In the impartiality of His
goodness God ordained all that's true. God says, "Let the person
who has ears sharp enough to hear invisible inner meanings love
My reflection and pant after My words. Let this person write My
words in his or her soul and conscience."

—Hildegard of Bingen, *Scivias*—

God let her hear these words in her soul, "From now on,
don't look at anything but love. Fix your eyes on love. No matter
what happens to you or others—within or without—look on
love alone. And live."

—Catherine of Genoa, *Vita*—

125

There are sixteen kinds of love:

Extravagant love comes from holy mercy and drives out empty honor and dysfunctional sickness.

True love comes from divine wisdom, brings satisfaction, and drives out disgusting lust.

Humble love comes only from holy simplicity and conquers pride. It drives the soul towards holy knowledge.

Constant love comes from good manners and never lies.

Great love comes from bold actions and finds wisdom for itself in all things.

Love that has discovered God's intimacy stuns the earth with its effortless kindness.

Disciplined love and holy habits never rest, but they are comfortable with themselves.

The love that permeates comes from an overabundance, but it lies completely still and finds all things tasteless, except God.

The love that is impatient for good reasons cries out for good, and is never silent. This love is happy and never guilt-ridden.

The love that understands God's teachings loves children, while beautiful love rejuvenates the soul, even though the body ages and becomes old.

Exquisite love gives innocence and erases every complaint of the grumbling heart, and powerful love pleases God.

Above all, the bright love that floods the soul with sweet pain causes her to die without death.

And the fiery love that comes from great strength is something that nobody can understand.

—Mechthild of Magdeburg—
The Flowing Light of the Godhead

june 8 🌿

You, God, are a fire that always burns without consuming. You are a fire consuming in its heat every compartment of the soul's self-absorbed love. You are a fire lifting all chill and giving all light. In Your light You show me Your truth. You're the Light that outshines every light.

You, God, give the mind's eye Your divine light so completely and excellently, You bring lucidity even to the light of faith. In that faith, I see my soul has life, and in that light, I receive You who are Light itself.

—Catherine of Siena, *Dialogue*—

june 9 🌿

Who am I? None other than the Supreme Good. I give you all good things when you seek me conscientiously.

Whom do you believe Me to be? I am God, above all things and in all things, but you want to treat Me as a serf who fears his lord. How? You want Me to do *your* will. You want to ignore My teachings.

I don't remember a beginning, and I don't fear any end. The heavens contemplate Me. They vibrate with My praises and obey Me in the integrity with which I created them. I designed the sun, the moon, and the stars, and they rise and set in the heavens on their proper courses, while blasts of wind and rain occur when I direct them to. All do the bidding of their Creator.

—Hildegard of Bingen, *Scivias*—

june 10 🌿

Truly the light of God is a sea because it nourishes my soul. And it's a peaceful sea, Eternal Trinity. Its waters move in tranquility, and my soul is not afraid because in this sea of light I know what Is.

God is a bright ocean that distills and reveals hidden truths so that my soul has a better understanding of how to trust Love, and this water is a mirror in which You, Eternal Trinity, give me knowledge. When I look in this mirror—holding it in the hand of love—I see myself.

I see that I'm Your creation, and I see that I'm in You while You're in me through the union You achieved between Your Godhead and our humanity. This light shows You, God, to me. In this light I know You.

—Catherine of Siena, *Dialogue*—

june 11 🌿

That I love you is not a question. I, God, love you passionately because I am love itself. I love you all the time because I want to be loved passionately Myself. I love you forever because I'm eternal. My love has no end, and My love has no beginning, either.

—Mechthild of Magdeburg—
The Flowing Light of the Godhead

Always love your soul and always love the souls of your neighbors. Always be eager to follow through on whatever you promise God. And may the Lord be with you always, and may you always be with God. Amen.

—Clare of Assisi, *Blessing*—

june 12 🌿

Lord, You're my lover,
my desire,
my clear and flowing fountain,
and my sun.

You are the One
who teaches me
by loving me

unconditionally
just how I am to love.

And I?
I am Your reflection.

—Mechthild of Magdeburg—
The Flowing Light of the Godhead

june 13

Love said to me, "I don't like your cruelty to others, and unless you start being compassionate and kind, you'll soon find yourself robbed of my mercy. Sometimes your bad attitude makes you say hateful words, and if you're not careful, these may be followed often enough by murder.

"Other times, your insolence leads to your being abusive, and you become a horrible monster, poisoning not only one or two but anyone who might come near you in love or fellowship."

—Catherine of Siena, *Dialogue*—

june 14

Paul exhorts the Philippians that they should do all that has to be done, and not to complain about it.

Humanity stands at a crossroads. If—in the light—we seek salvation and healing from God, there's no doubt we'll receive it. But, as the apostle Paul says, we mustn't grouse. If we stop complaining and don't sin, we'll become complete in our human nature.

And please don't argue, either. But do show your loyalty to God. If you are kind and harm no one, you'll live a life without bitterness. You'll live as God's children in the simplicity and joy of your good actions.

—Hildegard of Bingen, *Book of Divine Works*—

june 15

Eternal Truth says, "It's true—Love has as many offshoots as a tree has branches. What gives life to both the tree and its branches, though, is the root, as long as the root is planted in the soil of humility. Humility is the governess and wet nurse of the love into which the branch of discernment is grafted. The source of humility—as I've already told you—is the soul's true knowledge of herself and My goodness.

"That's why wisdom is only good when it's rooted in humility. When wisdom is rooted in humility, it produces an overabundance of life-giving fruit for every one of its neighbors."

—Catherine of Siena, *Dialogue*—

If you really want to improve your life,
look to your Bridegroom,
Lord of the whole world.
Look and see how handsome God was as He stood there
richly attired in bloody red,
black and blue after His scourging,
bound to the cross.
Look and see how God received many gaping wounds for
you,
for love of you.
Take these to heart.

Then you'll be able to escape the world's dishonesty.
If you want to continue to grow,
look up and see
how your Bridegroom stood there on the cross
before the world's eyes,
blood running down Him, all over the ground.
God's bloody clothes will become your favorite thing to wear.

—Mechthild of Magdeburg—
The Flowing Light of the Godhead

Kiss your Lover before everything else.
God gives you every pleasure, absolutely.
Thank him for wanting to die because He loves you so
amazingly.
Don't let anyone mislead you, and
then you'll be queen of your Lover's kingdom forever.

If you choose this Goodness,
you'll rise—in joy—above the pain of this world.
See? Look at the sharp crown of thorns
God wore there on His head.
Admit your sins with a sad face,
and you will gain a deep knowledge of our joyous God.

—Mechthild of Magdeburg—
The Flowing Light of the Godhead

If you want real peace, raise the eye of your understanding
(which is true desire) and meet the exquisite look of divine
Love. God has always looked on us in love. God looked on us
lovingly long ago and still looks on us lovingly today, right
now.

God looked into His heart long ago and fell so much in love with us that He created us out of sheer love. Love, you see, is the explanation of all that's Good.

—Catherine of Siena, *Letters*—

june 19 🌿

Look at the amazing friendship our considerate Lord offers us! God's tenderness protects us while we're sinning, and He even pats us secretly and shows us our sins by the gentle light of His sweet mercy and grace. When we see ourselves so soul-dirty, we think God's mad at us, and we're encouraged by the Holy Spirit to feel godly sorrow and to pray.

At that point, we want nothing more than to change ourselves and make God happy. We hope God has forgiven us, and of course God has. Then our considerate Lord shows Himself to the soul. God is happy. The Lord's face is the most cheerful one you'll ever see. He welcomes the soul as a friend. God welcomes our souls as if they had been in pain and prison, which they have.

Our considerate Lord then says, "Sweetheart, I'm glad you came to Me when you were hurting so. Know I've always been with you. Now you see Me. Now you see how much I love you. Now we are made one in bliss."

That's how I came to understand that everything is made available to us through God's unending goodness.

—Julian of Norwich, *Revelations*—

june 20 🌿

God said, "When you are self-absorbed, you rob your neighbors of true love and affection. Self-absorption is the foundation and very essence of all evil. Every crime, hatred, cruelty, and ugliness comes from the root of self-absorbed love. It poisons the whole world.

"Self-absorbed love has even sickened the mystic body of the holy Church and the universal body of Christianity. Remember, all integrity is built on a love for your neighbors.

"Remember the truths I've taught you: Love gives life to every virtue. Nothing good can exist without agape love. In other words, virtuous living is only possible through a genuine love for Me."

—Catherine of Siena, *Dialogue*—

june 21 🌿

Thinking is no longer important to me,
nor working, nor speaking.
When Love takes me up high,
thought loses its meaning.
Love looks at me with her divine eyes
and I lose my self-directed goals.
Thought becomes nothing to me,
or work, or talk,
where all is Love.

—Marguerite Porete, *The Mirror of Simple Souls*—

Help me please You
in humility of spirit,
in brotherly and sisterly love,
in pure simplicity,
in humble shyness,
in cleanliness of heart,
in the protection of my senses,
in appreciation of life,
in alacritous obedience,
in sweet patience,
in spiritual discipline,
in a chosen poverty,
in holy tolerance,
in maturity of conduct,
in cheerfulness of spirit,
in all truth,
in good conscience,
in steadiness of faith,
in godly perseverance,
in strength of hope,
in the wholeness of loving,
and in the joyful harmony of Your kindness,
so the prickly thorn bush of my heart will be changed into a
paradise of good acts and a red raspberry bush of total
spiritual excellence, as if it were a field full of everything
peaceful, holy, loving, and kind, all blessed by God!

—Gertrude the Great, *Spiritual Exercises*—

136

Gentle Truth told me, "I've shown you, my dearest daughter, that on earth guilt isn't atoned for by suffering simply as suffering. Only suffering accepted with longing, love, and heartfelt contrition counts. The value isn't in the suffering, but in the soul's desire.

"Also, neither desire nor any other virtue has any value except through My only-begotten Son—Christ crucified—because the soul gains life and love from Him. Any virtue is only a following in Christ's footsteps. This is the single way suffering is of value; only then it makes amends for sin.

"Gentle, unifying love accomplishes this, and this love is born from the sweet knowledge of My goodness and from the godly contrition the heart discovers when it knows itself and recognizes its own sins. Such knowledge gives birth to a real animosity for sin and for the soul's self-absorbed sensuality. It also produces a vibrant humility.

"So you see that those who feel genuine contrition, a love for true patience, and humility suffer without impatience. That's how they atone for the times their lives fall short of the mark of spiritual excellence."

—Catherine of Siena, *Dialogue*—

Love says, "God commands us to love Him with all our heart and soul and strength, and God commands us to love ourselves as we should, and then our neighbors as ourselves.

"First, we are to love God with all our heart. That means our thoughts should always be in God.

"We must also love God with all our soul. That means until death we must speak nothing but the truth.

"We must also love God with all our strength. That means everything we do each day, we do only for the Lord.

"We must also love ourselves as we're commanded. That means we must focus—not on our own self-interests—but on God's will.

"We must also love our neighbors as ourselves. That means we shouldn't act, think, or speak towards our neighbors in any way that we wouldn't want them to act, think, or speak towards us.

"These instructions are necessary for salvation and healing. Nobody can gain grace any other way."

—Marguerite Porete, *The Mirror of Simple Souls*—

My strong angels, be with me wherever I go and guard me wherever I am. Keep my enemies from my front door. Stand before me with your sword because you were picked to be my guardian angels when time began. Always protect me well against my enemies.

Stand at the first gate with your sword in your right hand. Keep this entrance closed to proud, lazy words. When they want to leave my mouth, don't let them. Sharpen my tongue like a hoe, so it can dig up vices and plant virtues, to the praise and glory of the highest Emperor and His mother.

Do the same thing with your holy fingers. Put two seals of love on my eyes, to improve my sight. Don't let my eyes see and lust after the distractions this world offers. Always keep my vision open and alert.

Also keep me vigilant, so my sleepiness doesn't interrupt the worship of the divine office, and so my mind doesn't get weary praising God, His mother, the angels in their special places up in heaven, and everyone else there.

Put your hands over my ears in the name of Jesus. Don't let one harmful word gain access to them and carry poison to my soul.

Put my feet in chains of love. Don't let them walk in the way of spiritual error, and then my every step will honor Christ and His mother.

—Umiltà of Faenza, *Sermons*—

O Love! Let my Jesus hang dead before my eyes.

Dead, plainly dead, that I might live more abundantly.
Dead that the Father might adopt me more dearly as His
child.
Dead that I might live more happily.

Dearest Death, you're the happiest thing I possess. Let
my soul find a home for itself in you, Death, for you grow the
fruits of eternal life. Help me hope beneath your wings forever.

Saving Death, may my soul hang out in your very bright
goodness. Most valuable Death, you're my dearest ransom.
Life-giving Death, I want to melt beneath your wings. Death,
dewdrop of life, may the very sweet spark of life you bring
burn in me forever.

—Gertrude the Great, *Spiritual Exercises*—

Eternal Strength!
In Your very heart You planned all Creation
and put everything in order.
Through Your Word, all things are still created
however You wish.

Your very own Word even took
on flesh and knew the form
we inherited from Adam—
that earthly form
our disobedience stained—
and that's how sorrow was removed
from the most intimate clothes humanity wears.

How great is the kindness of the One who saves!
God frees all things by becoming one with human life.
Your divinity—free of sinful chains—breathed
life into compassion,
removing sadness from the most
intimate clothes humanity wears.

Glory to the Father and the Son and the Holy Spirit.
God removed sadness from the most intimate clothes we
wear.

—Hildegard of Bingen, *Book of Divine Works*—

june 28 🌿

I am the least, the weakest, the most common person on
earth, Lord, and I beg You, my heavenly Father, Christ, Spirit,
Holy Trinity, to forgive me today of all my sins of omission,
committed in Your holy service. Forgive not only those sins I
committed while seeking to improve my life, or out of necessity,

but also those that I committed because of sinful spite, which I could have easily stopped if I'd just felt like it.

Please accept, Lord, this tiny improvement in my will, and help me change what in me is spiritually stupid because I want to lead a holy life and have community with Your saints on earth.

—Mechthild of Magdeburg—
The Flowing Light of the Godhead

june 29 ❦

The first step to spiritual excellence is an awareness of sinfulness.
The second step is confession of sins, and grieving—feeling shameful and bitter.
The third step is grief-stricken penance.
And the fourth step is an awareness of God's mercy.
The fifth step is a knowledge of self.

Remember that each of these steps takes time and can't be rushed. Yes, it's heartbreaking that the soul must move painfully slowly toward God. It takes such baby steps. I myself spent much time weeping at each step, with bitter comfort.

The sixth step is the turning point. Illumination happens. My soul was gifted then with a more profound awareness of my sins. And I prayed with my soul on fire in love.

The seventh step was the gift of grace to look on the cross of Christ's death. I didn't like doing this because it made me terribly sad.

The eighth step brought me home. While looking at the cross, I was given an even better understanding of the way God's Son died for our sins. This understanding set my soul so on fire that I took off all my clothes and offered my whole person to God.

The ninth step took me further on my way, which is the way of the cross. I found refuge—like all sinners do—at the foot of the cross, and to stand there I had to forgive everyone who'd ever hurt me. I had to strip myself of every worldly pleasure and possession. I had to give up all attachments to men and women, friends and family, and everyone else. I had to relinquish possession even of my own self. Then I was free.

The tenth step is when I asked God how I could continue to make Him happy. Then the Lord—crucified on the cross and merciful—revealed Himself to me often, when I was asleep and awake, and He told me to look at His wounds: "I suffered all these painful things for *you*."

—Angela of Foligno, *Memorial*—

The Soul says to God:

"Lord, You love me so much! You help me persevere in hunger and thirst, in working and pleasure, until that playful hour of mystical union, when from Your divine mouth the special words—no one else hears—flow. These words bind me to You.

"Nobody but the soul who strips herself of earth and puts her ear next to Your mouth hears these special words. How she appreciates Your joy and treasures Your love. Thank you!"

—Mechthild of Magdeburg—
The Flowing Light of the Godhead

j u l y

july 1 🔥

O Holy Power who forged the Way for us!
You penetrate all in heaven and earth and even down below.
You're everything in One.
Through You, clouds billow and roll, and winds fly!
Seeds drip juice,
springs bubble out into brooks, and
spring's refreshing greens flow—through You—over all the earth!
You also lead my spirit into Fullness.

Holy Power, blow wisdom in my soul
and—with your wisdom—Joy!

—Hildegard of Bingen, *Hymn*—

july 2 🌿

In the light of my growing trust in You, I gain wisdom through the wisdom of the Word, Your Son. In this light, I'm strong and steady. I persevere. This illumination gives me hope. This divinely confident light won't let me collapse along the journey. Instead, it teaches me the way. Without this light, I'd be walking in the dark. That's why I asked You, Eternal Father, to enlighten me with the light of the most holy hope in You.

—Catherine of Siena, *Dialogue*—

july 3 🌿

When anger tries to burn up the temple of my body, I'll look to the goodness of God, whom anger never touched. I'll look to God whom anger never touched, and I'll become sweeter than the breeze whose gentleness moistens the earth. I'll look to God whom anger never touched, and I'll have spiritual joy because virtues will begin to show themselves in me. I'll look to God whom anger never touched, and—because I look to Him—I'll experience God's calm goodness.

—Hildegard of Bingen, *Scivias*—

july 4 🌿

Love God's goodness in yourself. Love His immeasurable love. You'll find both of these—God's goodness and His endless love—in the cell of self-knowledge. In this cell you'll find God because—just as God holds within Himself everything that's alive—you'll find within yourself memory, which holds and is perfectly capable of possessing the treasure of God's blessing.

That's where you'll also find understanding. When we understand and know God's will, we can share in the wisdom of God's Son. The divine will wants nothing else but for us to be made holy. When we see this truth, our souls can never be sad or shaken—no matter what happens—because then we'll know everything is done with God's blessing, and tremendous love.

—Catherine of Siena, *Letters*—

july 5 🌿

I don't think we can have virtue or the fullness of grace if we don't live in the cell of our heart and soul. Only in this inner private place do we gain the treasure that is life and health for us. Here in this secret place we're given the sacred nothingness that is a holy, intimate knowledge of ourselves and of God. The physician Luke told us in his Gospel that God alone is the One who is good.

—Catherine of Siena, *Letters*—

149

If God is good, why do you put such puny value on knowing God's goodness, when this same goodness gave God's Son over to death to set you free from death, through Christ's great sadness and many labors?

When you say you can't do good works, you're just not telling the truth. You do have eyes to see with, ears to hear with, a heart to think with, hands to work with, and feet to walk with. Your body can stand up. It can lie down. It can sleep. It can wake. It can eat. It can fast.

God created you this way. So, resist the impulses of your flesh, and God will help you because when you set yourself against the devil like a strong warrior against his enemy, God delights in your struggle. God wants you to call on Him in every hour, in every trouble. God wants you to call on Him constantly.

—Hildegard of Bingen, *Scivias*—

God is as willing to save us as He is strong and wise. Christ Himself is the foundation of every Christian teaching, because Jesus showed us how to do good in return for evil. We see that God Himself is this love, and that God's Spirit treats us kindly, in the same way Jesus teaches us to act towards ourselves and others.

God wants us to be like Him in undiminished, unending love towards ourselves and our neighbors. God wants us to hate sin as He Himself hates it and to love the soul as He Himself loves it.

God brought these words to my mind, and they have been an endless strength to me: "I protect you *absolutely*."

—Julian of Norwich, *Revelations*—

july 8 🌿

Mary speaks: "When I was young, I suckled Jesus. Later, I suckled God's bride, holy Christianity.

"How? When I stood under the cross feeling lonesome and dead, as the sword of Jesus' physical suffering cut me open and wounded my soul, both my son's wounds and my breasts were opened then. His wounds bled, and my breasts flowed. This is how each soul came to be resuscitated and completely restored as Jesus poured the sparkling red wine into my red mouth."

—Mechthild of Magdeburg—
The Flowing Light of the Godhead

july 9 🌿

Stop being foolish! Get out of that filthy spiritual muck right now. You roll around in sensuality the way pigs roll in mud. But you can stop.

Abandon all cruelty, slander, hatred, spite, complaining, judgmental thoughts, and violence of every sort. Stop dabbling in stealing. Stop betraying. Stop enjoying the stupid pleasures of this world. Cut off pride's smirk.

Refuse the hatred you have in your heart for those who hurt you. Compare the harm you do to God and your neighbors with the hurt done to you, and you'll see that what you do to God and them is far worse than what is done to you. When you hide hatred in your heart, you insult Me, your God. You break My law then. And you hurt your neighbors by depriving them of love.

Remember? I commanded you to love Me above all things, and your neighbors as your very self. Notice I didn't qualify this statement. I didn't say, "If they hurt you, don't love them." NO. Your love must be free and genuine because I gave this command. I gave this command, and it's the Truth. Obey it with the same sincerity with which I gave it because—if you don't—you're just hurting your own self and harming your soul by robbing yourself of the life of grace.

—Catherine of Siena, *Dialogue*—

july 10 ❧

My soul held a conversation with her Lover, and she used many kind words to thank Him for the unsurpassed gifts received from the hands of God:

"Lord, Your generosity feeds my marvelous body in the best of ways.

152

"Your mercy comforts my soul marvelously.

"And Your comforting love puts my entire being at ease for all eternity!"

—Mechthild of Magdeburg—
The Flowing Light of the Godhead

july 11 🍂

God says, "Each soul happily accepting My yoke of obedience and truth lives with a pure heart and absolutely gains My unlimited and ineffable love. Through the light of trusting in God and in the blood of the Lamb, your soul will better understand Me. You will see your own inability to respond to Me in the excellent manner Love deserves. At that point, My light will help you to start seeking how and where you can better pay your debt to Me.

"Then you'll trample your own weaknesses underfoot. You'll eradicate your own self-absorbed will. Your search will lead you by the light of trust to a spiritually disciplined, joyful lifestyle."

—Catherine of Siena, *Dialogue*—

july 12 🌿

Ignore honors, suffering, and possessions. Be sad after sinning. If someone honors you, you should feel uncomfortable. If someone makes you suffer, you should be glad. If someone does you a favor, you should be worried. If you sin against God or your neighbor, you should feel sad. If you can't feel sadness, then you must contemplate how deeply and how long I was saddened on account of you.

—Mechthild of Magdeburg—
The Flowing Light of the Godhead

july 13 🌿

God, we are tired of our stubborn hearts, but we sure don't know what to do about them. Somehow stop our insensitivity. Transform these rockhard feelings that I hold so close to my chest. Melt my stony heart in the hot, overflowing blood of Your Son because the warmth of that priceless blood is enough to dissolve any heart's stone-like frigidity. Melt this boulder in my chest. All this and more is exactly what the Holy Spirit does when He enters the soul.

—Catherine of Siena, *Letters*—

A servant stands respectful before her lord, ready to do the master's will. The lord looks on the servant with love—sweetly, gently—and sends her to a certain place to do his will. And the servant doesn't just go—she dashes off, running as fast as possible.

She loves doing the lord's will but soon falls into a small valley and is hurt badly. Groaning and moaning and tossing about and writhing, she can't rise or help herself.

In all this, the greatest hurt I saw this servant suffering was that she couldn't be consoled. The servant couldn't turn her face to look on the most loving lord, who was very close to her and in whom is all consolation, but like a person who was momentarily extremely weak and irrational, the servant only noticed her painful feelings and on-going distress.

In this trauma the servant suffered seven great hurts: severe bruising, clumsiness of body, weakness, blindness of reason and confusion of mind (so much so that she'd almost forgotten the master's love), paralysis, loneliness, and the uncomfortable fact that the place where she lay was narrow and painful.

The servant had nobody to help her, so she just lay there. I was amazed that this servant could suffer all this woe so submissively. I looked carefully and saw no fault in her, for the only reason this servant fell was her good will and great desire to serve the lord.

—Julian of Norwich, *Revelations*—

july 15 🔥

O, Obedience, always joyous! You don't make ugly, impatient faces. You preserve your beauty with the pleasantness of waiting. You stay totally, powerfully serene. Your perseverance is impressive. You're so strong, you reach from heaven to earth. You unlock heaven.

You're a pearl hidden and unknown. The world tramples on you and never notices you.

You humble yourself in submission to others. Your authority never ends. Nobody's your boss. You've turned your back on lesser things like self-absorbed pleasures. You have got dignity because you've conquered many enemies and gained your freedom.

—Catherine of Siena, *Dialogue*—

july 16 🔥

Do you want to know how you can best use God's holy favor and enjoy it as He wants you to? You know God's will will teach you this itself, if you welcome it. Receive God's kindness externally (via virtues) and internally (through your yearnings). Respect it humbly. Never let go of it.

Be submissive when things go wrong in your life. Give God's kindness time and room in you. That's all it asks. Then it will melt you so deeply into God, you'll know what God's will is: You'll understand how long you should look for His intense caresses, and you'll know how and when to act kindly to your neighbors.

When you've succeeded in this in your most intimate being, your soul will grow tired in the embrace of her mortal body. Then the soul will say after each pleasurable encounter with God:

"Lord, now leave my inner self
and stand by my earthly self,
so all my actions will shine
in proportion to Your favor.

"Help me suffer willingly
and complain very little about my problems."

—Mechthild of Magdeburg—
The Flowing Light of the Godhead

july 17 🌿

The angels praise God obediently. They use their voices and their lyres to praise God's creation. Those of us on earth must also worship God in two ways. First, we should praise Him, and second, we should do good works.

God is known by our praise, and God's miracles are seen in our acts of kindness because we're filled with His love and are happy to be doing the Lord's work diligently. All of God's miracles are accomplished through our praise and through our kindnesses.

—Hildegard of Bingen, *The Book of the Rewards of Life*—

july 18 ❦

God says, "You'll learn that all suffering here on earth is small because time is small. Time is no bigger than the point of a needle. When time is over, so is suffering.

"Now do you see how very small your suffering is? With that in mind, endure it patiently. The thorns you pass through here can't touch your heart. Why? As far as self-absorbed love is concerned, your heart has been drawn away from yourself, and it is firmly joined to Me by the most compelling, most intimate love."

—Catherine of Siena, *Dialogue*—

july 19 ❦

God gives us what we want when our good actions mirror God's good intent. That's why every kindness we do has the sweetest aroma to God. Remember that in the Old Testament God was in no way pleased with the sacrificed blood of goats. Remember that He spurned that sort of phony offering and demanded a genuine spirit from those who love Him.

Remember how pleased God was, however, with the genuine good will of those who say, "We love you, God."

—Hildegard of Bingen, *The Book of the Rewards of Life*—

In my vision I saw something small. No bigger than a hazelnut, it lay in the palm of my hand, round as a ball. Looking at it with the eye of my understanding, I wondered, "What is that?" I was given to understand it is everything in creation. That this minute thing lasted at all amazed me. It was so tiny, it looked like it would suddenly vanish into nothing.

Concerning this tiny, hazelnut-sized cosmos, I received this answer in my soul, "It lasts and always will because God loves it." I saw then that everything's alive through God's love. The little thing I saw that seemed like it could vanish into nothingness because of its insubstantiality, this little thing is why our hearts and souls don't know perfect peace.

We seek rest here in this very little thing, in which there is no rest, and we don't know our God, who is almighty, all wise, and all good—God is the only true Rest. That's why no soul is at rest until it scorns as nothing all created things.

When the soul becomes the nothing God wants the soul to be—for love—when it wants instead to possess the Lord, who is everything, then it can accept spiritual rest.

—Julian of Norwich, *Revelations*—

july 21 🌿

The Lord revealed to me that I would sin. When I realized this, I felt a sort of gentle fear, and the Lord answered this fear: "I protect you. I'll keep you safe." God said this to me with more love and assurance than I can possibly tell you.

But, still, you shouldn't start thinking, "Well, since God loves me, it's okay to sin so I can get more reward." Beware of this thought. Hate it. It comes from the devil.

—Julian of Norwich, *Revelations*—

july 22 🌿

Be kind to those who treat you badly, who talk about you or hurt you physically. Don't be reactive. Respond to them calmly, on your own terms. Ignore the injury. Let them go on their way. With a calm exterior and a peaceful soul we must exercise kindness to those who hurt us and insult us. We must be willing to kiss the feet of the person who treats us badly.

How do we learn to do this? Look at Christ. See how He endured the bitter abuse hurled at Him. Jesus endured everything with kindness. Christ's example strengthens us. It helps us not hold a grudge.

Finally, we must also imitate Christ in being honest in everything we say and do. We ourselves must not be mean or mendacious.

—Angela of Foligno, *Instructions*—

july 23 🌿

One day God spoke to me and I heard these words, "You won't be overcome." God wants us to pay attention to His words. God wants us to be strong in our certainty in Him, always, both in good times and in bad. The Lord loves us, and God so enjoys our company.

God loves being with us and wants us to love Him and enjoy being with Him and trust Him completely, and all will be well.

—Julian of Norwich, *Revelations*—

july 24 🌿

Be strong. Watch out for the sly serpent's traps. He lies in ambush for your heel. Those who envy you set many snares for you. Know for a fact that those who put traps out for you will fall into them themselves, however. Daughter of Jerusalem, go ahead and walk with a joyful heart in the way of contemplation of the Lord.

Run the course well. Run it lovingly. Run it purely. Run it with discretion and humility.

—Elisabeth of Schönau, *Letters*—

Happy is the person
who clings with all their heart to our Lord
and shares in God's sacred banquet.

God is the one whose beauty is praised by heaven's
indefatigable angels.
God is the one whose kindness electrifies,
whose contemplation refreshes,
whose love satisfies,
whose joy replenishes,
whose celebration illuminates the world,
whose fragrance resurrects the dead,
whose splendid vision blesses,
whose eternal glory shines,
whose everlasting light burns brightest,
whose mirror reflects all things flawlessly.

Look in that Mirror each and every day.
Study your face in it forever.
Then you can put on the most beautiful clothes
and wear them and every one of virtue's flowers
because happy poverty, holy humility, and indescribable
kindness
are reflected in that Mirror
as you contemplate them there.

—Clare of Assisi, *Letters*—

july 26 🌿

You are my Mother, and more than my Mother. My earthly mother was in labor a day or a night delivering me, but You, my beautiful, sweet Lord, were in labor for me over thirty years. How You labored in love for me Your whole life. But when it came Your time to deliver me, Your labor pains were so terrible that Your sacred sweat fell on the earth in huge drops of blood. When the hour came for You to deliver me, You were placed on the hard bed of the cross—Your nerves and all Your veins ruptured.

Surely it's no surprise Your veins burst when in a single day You gave birth to the whole world.

—Marguerite d'Oingt, *Page of Meditation*—

july 27 🌿

I'm in harmony with the God-Man nearly always. It all started one day when I was given a new confidence that there's no mediator between God and myself. Since then, both night and day I've known the joy of Christ's humanity.

Right now I'd like to sing and praise Him:
"I praise You, God, my Sweetheart!
I make Your cross my bed.
Under my head I pull poverty for my pillow,
and the other parts of the bed

163

are the suffering and scorn I've found to rest on."

—Angela of Foligno, *Memorial*—

july 28 🌿

In my vision, the man with the golden head and fine white hair is Christ, of course. The golden head is Christ's divinity; the apostle Paul tells us in his first letter to the Corinthians that Christ's head is God. The bride in the Song of Songs refers to this head by saying that his head is the best gold. That the fine hair of his head is like pure white wool refers to the angels, who from the beginning of time preserved their innocence because they followed God in unending contemplation and rooted themselves in His unceasing love like hair is rooted in the head.

Divine wisdom's most excellent thoughts are also like white hair, and the prophet Isaiah describes these when he quotes the Lord as saying that his thoughts aren't like our thoughts. The thoughts of the Lord order all things in tranquility. Last, the beautiful, flashing eyes of the man in my vision are the mercy and truth that come from Christ's face. They run through all His works, as the psalmist reminds us that all the Lord's ways are mercy and truth.

—Elisabeth of Schönau, *Third Book of Visions*—

Love also says, "Kindness towards others obeys no created thing but Love. Kindness towards others possesses nothing of her own, and if she does possess something, she never says it belongs to her. Kindness towards others skips her own needs to help a neighbor. Kindness towards others asks no payment from anyone for any good or any pleasure she does. Kindness towards others knows no guilt, fear, or anxiety. She is so good, no circumstances can break her spirit.

"Kindness towards others doesn't think this world is worth much, really. Kindness towards others gives to her neighbors all she has that's worth anything. She keeps nothing for herself. Her amazing generosity often makes her promise what she doesn't have because she knows the more she gives, the more she receives in her soul. Kindness towards others is such a wise businesswoman that she earns profits everywhere when others go out of business, and she escapes all those things that bind others. That's how she has such influence and such wealth, because she pleases Love.

"Remember, if we want to love others well, we must be humble in spirit as we are being kind to our neighbors."

—Marguerite Porete, *The Mirror of Simple Souls*—

july 30 🕯

Choose Christ as your life model. Choose the suffering God-Man. Learn from His life. Learn excellence from Christ. Listen to His teachings. Take all your desire and chase God down with it. Work to reach his cross.

See how Christ gave Himself as an example. Jesus told us to look at Him with the eyes of our souls. God said: "Learn from me. I am gentle. My soul is humble. You'll find rest for your hearts here."

Pay attention to what Christ didn't say. He didn't say, "Learn to fast from Me" or "Learn to scorn the world and live in poverty" or "Learn from Me how to perform great miracles," although He did each of these things well. No, instead Jesus said, "Learn from Me because I am gentle and humble in My soul."

The point is that Christ made humility and gentleness the foundation for every other virtue. Nothing else matters. Not integrity, not fasting, not poverty, not shabby clothing, not years of good works, not the accomplishment of miracles—none of these is important without a humble heart.

—Angela of Foligno, *Instructions*—

july 31 🕯

God's mercy is kind. God gives divine, abundant grace to those who love Him. God's limitless goodness has comforted me, his servant, and—look!—the Lord's hands are still reaching out to comfort me.

No one can stop God's mercy, not even those who think too highly of themselves, not even those who sneer at whatever they think is weaker than they are, not even those who disrespect God's riches. How I hope these words will instruct the minds of those who are humble.

—Elisabeth of Schönau, *Second Book of Visions*—

august

august 1

Don't set your heart on something less valuable than you yourself are. If you do that, you surrender your dignity because—remember—people come to resemble what they love. If I love sin, which is nothingness, I too become a nothing. I can't fall any lower than that.

Sin begins simply, innocuously. It begins in loving what God hates and hating what God loves. That's why if you love the transient things of this world and yourself with a self-absorbed love, you sin. God hates this.

In fact, it makes God so unhappy, He decided to work out vengeance and punishment for it on His own body. God made Himself an anvil and on this anvil hammered out our sins.

—Catherine of Siena, *Letters*—

august 2 ❦

God is your way of life and your language. Anyone who wants to speak to you must learn this language of tranquility, and if they won't, beware of learning theirs. It may lead you to hell. Don't worry then if they look down on you.

I myself know from experience how bad it is for the soul to mimic the language of the world. Avoid it at all costs. Why? Because as one language is learned, the other is forgotten. Out goes peace and quiet for the soul and in comes a wearying restlessness. I only wish I could write with both of my hands, so I wouldn't forget one thing while I'm writing down another!

—Teresa of Avila, *The Way of Perfection*—

august 3 ❦

At one time my mind was led down to the bottom of the sea. There I saw hills and green valleys covered with moss, seaweed, and gravel. I understood this vista to mean that a person would be safe in body and soul—even in deep water—if they could see and understand God is always with us, *all the time*.

They would also feel more comfort than this whole world can offer, because God wants us to believe we see Him all the time, even though sometimes what we see of God is very little.

Little by little, God grows us ever more in grace, because God wants to be seen and sought. God wants to be awaited and trusted.

—Julian of Norwich, *Revelations*—

august 4 🌿

I begged God to let me know, if it were His will, could I please stop writing. Why? Well, I know I'm just as weak and undeserving—and more so—than I was thirty years ago when God commanded I should begin.

When I said to our Lord, "Can't I please stop writing?" He showed me a little sack in His hand and said to me, "I still have healing herbs."

I said, "But, Lord, I don't know any of those herbs."

The Lord answered me, "When you see them, though, you'll recognize them alright. With these, you can refresh the sick, strengthen the healthy, wake up the dead, and bless the good."

That's why I don't dare claim credit—no, not at all—for anything I say about love. It's God who reaches through me faithfully and makes empty hearts full.

—Mechthild of Magdeburg—
The Flowing Light of the Godhead

august 5 🌿

The psalmist tells us be happy in the Lord and He'll give us whatever our heart desires. What does this psalm teach us? You who believe in God day in and day out and who do good works loyally for God must also let yourselves experience and give in to the joy of virtue. Be happy in the One who is Lord of the universe.

Continue to follow Him steadily. Love the One who is your Creator. After you become happy in God, He'll give you everything good. Life. Whatever you're looking for and whatever your heart most wants. Your trust in God permits only those things that are good to search you out.

Contemplation teaches spiritual confidence and pursues only what pleases God. So complain to God as much as you need to. Don't forget to cry out to God on behalf of your needy brother and sister. Then the aroma of good deeds—through God's love in you—rises, and God never stops fulfilling the requests you make out of kindness. A dependable person pays attention to these things and remembers them well.

—Hildegard of Bingen, *The Book of the Rewards of Life*—

august 6 ❦

The loving Soul starts lamenting misery she can't bear: "I'm lovesick and my body's weak. Every day is stressful and hard because I suffer severely. My suffering makes the way long between my dear Lord and myself. Lover, how can I do without You for such a long time? Help me! I'm terribly far, too far away from You! Lord, if You don't hear my complaint and respond, I'll be forced once again to take up my sorrow and wait and suffer inside and out. Lord—dear Lord—You know so well how much I long to be with You."

Our Lord hears and answers, "When I come, I come as the Magnificent. I come as the All-Powerful. I come in all majesty when I come. Remember this and know it well. There's *never* been a grief so great I couldn't heal it completely. You must wait some more."

—Mechthild of Magdeburg—
The Flowing Light of the Godhead

august 7 🌿

Many think that the way of a Christian is hard, but God said to me, "Imitating Christ's Passion really isn't that difficult. It may seem to be, but it's not. It's easy for those for whom Christ died, to die for Him. It's easy for those for whom Christ suffered, to suffer for Him. It's easy for those for whom Christ was scorned, to be scorned for Him. It's easy for those who are loved by Christ, to love others for Him."

Because God is love, so can we be.

—Angela of Foligno, *Instructions*—

august 8 🌿

The soul is just like a house-husband who tidies up his house and puts everything in order. He sees to it that nothing damages it, and his provision for the future is always done wisely. He knows exactly what he's doing. He buys and tosses out, and does what's needed, and avoids making mistakes, and always knows how everything should be done.

That's exactly how it is with the soul. The soul is all about love, and love rules in the soul—mighty and powerful—working and resting, doing and not doing. Everything in the soul and everything coming to the soul follow love's will. Like fish swim in the immense sea and rest in its depths, and birds climb boldly through the air, so the soul feels its spirit moving freely through the enormous, profound, inexpressible riches of love.

—Beatrijs of Nazareth, *Seven Manners of Living*—

august 9 🌿

God guides his children along strange paths. The path of pain is a strange path. It is also a noble path and a holy path. God Himself walked it. Remember this.

On this path the soul aching for God is joyful because she remembers her sinless, guiltless Lord suffered much pain for His good deeds. Our dear Lord, the heavenly Father, delivered up His most beloved Son to be tortured, despite the fact that Jesus was absolutely innocent.

—Mechthild of Magdeburg—
The Flowing Light of the Godhead

Divine wisdom teaches much about poverty. Poverty shows us our flaws because we see how poor we are in our own beings. After this illumination, God's goodness becomes clear, and we love God's goodness without hesitating. And then we do spontaneous acts of kindness with God's good love. That's when all self-reliance is gone. When you possess this truth, no devil can ever trick you.

Poverty is the mother of all virtues. She's the one who teaches divine wisdom. The wise Son of God knew poverty. All His life the suffering God-Man knew only the poverty of the Cross. Christ's life began, continued, and ended on the cross. Jesus was always on the cross of poverty and constant pain and scorn and pure obedience. This is our heritage.

We must accept it as our birthright. Suffering lasts as long as you live, and the blessing is that there's only as much of it as you can bear. The more you mature, the more you love God, and the more you will try to do what the suffering God-Man does.

There's also another example of true poverty in the good thief crucified beside the God-Man. This thief had lived a crooked life, but once he accepted the divine light of God and saw God's goodness, he saw his own poverty immediately and accepted it.

That's why this thief scolded the other man being crucified (the one insulting Christ): "You're being crucified and yet you have no respect for God." He reminded the other that they were getting their just desserts, but He had done nothing wrong.

177

"Can't you see that?" he exhorted. Then he turned to Christ and asked Him to remember him when He entered His kingdom. He was saved then.

We sinners get no satisfaction—nor can we satisfy God—until we confess our absolute poverty to Him.

—Angela of Foligno, *Memorial*; *Instructions*—

august 11 🌿

God speaks: "When I looked and saw that humanity—whom I desperately loved—was paying no attention whatsoever to Me, My infinite goodness made Me put the key of obedience into the hand of My Truth—the gentle, loving Word. Then, My Son became the doorman who unlocked heaven's gate. Without this key and this lowly doorman (who is My Truth), nobody can enter.

"That's why Jesus said in the Gospel of John that nobody comes to the Father, but by Him. When Christ rose beyond all human companionship and ascended into heaven and back to Me, victorious, Jesus left you all this key of sweet obedience."

—Catherine of Siena, *Dialogue*—

When your body is touched and troubled by pain, it's like your soul is bathed in air and sunlight, coming to it through the painful body, and this gives the soul a wonderful clarity. The greater the pain, or the more general the suffering, the more purification or clarification goes on in the soul.

This is especially true of the painful problems of the heart. When these are endured, humbly and patiently, they give the soul a splendid luster, the nearer and better and closer they touch it. But remember that kind actions—more than anything else—cause the soul to shine with brilliance.

—Gertrude the Great, *The Herald of Divine Love*—

Everlasting God said, "Doing good to your neighbors proves your love for Me. And there's more. The virtue of patience in you is tested when your neighbors insult you. Your humility is tested by the proud. Your faith is tested by the unfaithful. Your hope is tested by the person who's hopeless. Your fairness is tested by the unreasonable. Your compassion is tested by the cruel. Your gentleness and kindness are tested by 'rage-oholics.' Your neighbors will test your goodness, and through these tests your virtues will be born and strengthened and grow."

—Catherine of Siena, *Dialogue*—

One day the scorching, reeking devil visited me and kept me busy. My encounter with Satan was disgusting and painful. The physical heat was oppressive, and I was frightened. That whole day in my head I heard chattering and talking, as if between two speakers both nattering on at once, conducting a confused debate. What an unearthly commotion it was!

The noise was so low I couldn't understand what they were saying, but it was all meant to make me lose hope. Still, I kept trusting in God. I spoke words out loud to console me. I fixed my eyes on the Lord's cross and received comfort. I kept my tongue busy speaking of Christ's Passion. I fixed my heart on God with all the trust and strength in me.

The devils kept me busy all that night and well into the morning, till a little after sunrise. Then all at once they disappeared, leaving nothing but their stench. That lingered for a while. But, because I'd despised them, I was delivered from them. The strength of Christ's Passion delivered me.

Miserable sin, what've you got to say for yourself? What are you? You're nothing. God is everything.

—Julian of Norwich, *Revelations*—

august 15 🌿

God says, "Come on a road trip with Me! This road makes such joy for those who travel on it that it turns every bitterness into sweetness for them, and every burden into something light. Though you're in the body's darkness, you'll find light. Though you're mortal, you'll find eternal life. Through love and the light of faith, you'll taste endless Truth, and I promise you refreshment in return for every present weariness you bear for Me.

"I'm grateful to you and I'm sensitive to your problems. I'm kind. I have good things for you. You could never describe, nor hear, nor see this joy possessed by those who travel this road. Along the way, even in this life, you taste some of the divine good prepared for you in everlasting life."

—Catherine of Siena, *Dialogue*—

august 16 🌿

God showed me two kinds of illness we tend to have. One is impatience, which we get when we complain and endure our pain awkwardly. The other is despair, which comes from the fear that originates in our lack of confidence in God.

God wants us cured of both of these. He most wants us to have confidence in His happiness and in His love. Love makes us accept power and wisdom humbly because we realize God in His kindness forgets our sins when we repent and wants us to do the same to ourselves, too.

The Lord wants us to forget our sins. He wants us to forget every bit of our depression. God wants us to forget each doubt and every fear.

—Julian of Norwich, *Revelations*—

august 17 🌿

Reason asks Love, "What should we call the Soul? Does she have a name?"

Love answers, "The Soul has twelve names. They are the Most Wonderful, the Not Understood, the Most Innocent of Jerusalem's Daughters, the Church's Foundation, the Illumination of Knowledge, the One Made Beautiful Through Loving, She Who Lives Through Praise, She Who Dies in Everything Through Humility, She Who Is Peaceful Through God's Will, She Who Is Willful in Nothing but in the Divine Will, the One Who Is Completely Satisfied in God's Goodness Through the Trinity, and her last name is this: Oblivion, Forgotten."

—Marguerite Porete, *The Mirror of Simple Souls*—

Lucifer, the "light-bringer"—thrust from divine glory because of his pride—was so mighty when first created that he fell into seeing himself as all-beautiful and all-powerful. As Satan looked in the mirror of his beauty and admired his super strength at length, he discovered pride and began to lust after his basest desires and believed he could succeed in his ill-fated coup. Lucifer eyed God's heavenly kingdom and pictured himself living and ruling there, where he could flaunt his beauty and strength.

Satan said to himself, "I'll shine in heaven just as God does," and his followers approved of his scheme, cheering him on: "What you want, we want." But when he began to carry out what he had long craved, the long arm of the Lord cast him down with all his faction into fiery blackness. God made Satan and his angels smolder instead of shine, and they lost their God-given brightness.

On the other hand, we mustn't forget that when Adam and Eve were expelled from Paradise, an amazing, shining splendor surrounded the Garden of Eden. This bright light foreshadowed that the transgression occurring in Paradise would one day be wiped out by God's unending mercy.

—Hildegard of Bingen, *Scivias*—

When I rejoice in the Lord, no one can rob me of this joy. Always rejoice in God, and neither bitterness nor depression can overcome you.

Let your mind look into the Spirit's eternal mirror.
Let your soul bathe in the Father's glorious light.
Let your heart contemplate the divine Son of God.

Contemplation will transform your whole self into the image of the Godhead, and you'll taste the sweetness hidden away by God Himself for those who love Him.

Totally love the Son who gave Himself completely for your love, and remember that the sun and moon admire the Son of the Most High, whose priceless gifts are endless.

—Clare of Assisi, *Letters*—

Lord Jesus Christ, Son of the living God,
help me—
in every need,
with all my heart
and a thirsty soul—

to reach for You,
and in You who are sweet and happy
may I find my rest.

With my whole spirit and self,
let me desire You,
for You're the only One who holds true happiness.
In Your priceless blood, Lord of mercy, write
Your wounds in my heart.
Help me read there both Your pain and love.
May the memory of Your wounds
forever remain in my heart's secret places,
kindling compassion in me.

Help me focus solely on You,
who are the sweetness of my heart.

—Gertrude the Great, *The Herald of Divine Love*—

august 21 🌾

I bless, encourage, and challenge you to a happy, holy patience. Without it, we can't please God.

Substitute patience for your angry fist, and you'll gain the fruit of your troubles. If enduring so much pain seems hard to you, remember three things, which will help you to endure things more patiently.

First, remember how short your life is. You can never be sure of tomorrow. Since time is short, shouldn't we suffer patiently?

Second, remember the fruit that follows your sufferings. Paul says there's no comparison between our sufferings and the reward of heavenly glory.

Third, remember that those who suffer angrily or impatiently lose both here and also eternally.

—Catherine of Siena, *Letters*—

august 22 ❦

Dear Jesus, I need to ask You something. I just can't stand it any longer because I see there's this terrible blindness at the bottom of my question, but here it is.

I've noticed religious people in particular rebuff Your divine confidences.

Here's how: I've seen Your divine heart shine with warm love, like a small spark landing on a cold, blessed soul, and I've seen this soul receive an abundance of You until her heart burns, her soul melts, and her eyes tear up, and I know You'd like to make this earthly person so heavenly that someone else will actually be able to see and love God in them.

But what I don't get is: I have also often seen this same blessed person say to You, God, "Go away. I'm much too busy for that."

—Mechthild of Magdeburg—
The Flowing Light of the Godhead

august 23 🌿

Consider the wheel Christ is holding in His left hand in my vision. The left hand of God is the earthly life the Lord has given us. God created a shining wheel for us in this world, and this shining wheel is the teaching of sacred Scripture. The Lord gave this teaching through Himself and His followers so it could illuminate a world shadowed by error and ignorance.

That's why the psalmist tells us that the teaching of the Lord is bright and enlightens the eyes. The different rainbow colors in the wheel are the many different benefits of grace, as taught by the Savior for the good of the church and published in the Scriptures of truth. These are the treasures that are in the left hand of Wisdom, the Son of God. The apostle Paul said that God's Son was made poor although He was rich so that by His poverty we who were impoverished could be made rich.

—Elisabeth of Schönau, *Third Book of Visions*—

august 24 🌿

Immediately, the eyes of my soul were opened, and in a vision I saw God's wholeness and the wholeness of creation. In the sea, and also in everything beyond the sea in outer space, I saw nothing but God's power and God's presence. It was totally indescribable. My soul was overcome with wonder at everything.

I shouted, "The world is pregnant with God!" That's when I understood how small creation is when the enormity of God is considered. God's power fills the sea and everything beyond it. His presence is everywhere.

Then the Lord told me, "I've just now shown you only a little bit of My strength."

—Angela of Foligno, *Memorial*—

august 25 🌿

May God grant you the same power of trust and perseverance as the Canaanite woman possessed. Her confidence in God was so strong that she won her daughter's release from the devil. And there's more.

God wanted to show how pleased He was with her, and He wanted to give her trust in the Lord credit for the victory. That's why Jesus told her that her wishes would come true for her daughter, as Matthew writes in his Gospel.

Splendid, glorious Virtue reveals the presence of divine love's fire within the soul because people trust and hope only in what they love. These three virtues—love, faith, and hope—flow from one another because there's no love without faith and no faith without hope. These are the three pillars supporting the castle of our soul.

—Catherine of Siena, *Letters*—

august 26 ❦

Please, Lord, love me passionately. Love me often. Love me long.

Your love is the key to me, and the more passionately You love me, the purer I become. My life becomes more genuine then.

The more you love me, the more beautiful I become in my thoughts; and the longer You love me, the holier I become while living on this earth.

Make me real.

—Mechthild of Magdeburg—
The Flowing Light of the Godhead

august 27 ❦

Sweet Christ, highest Love, have compassion for me. Don't abandon me. I take refuge in Your kindness, because You're my only certainty. You have all my hope. You're the only Person I can turn to at a time like this.

You could say You're not obligated to love me. I already know I deserve nothing. However, the wood of the cross sets me on fire. Your pierced hands make visible Your generosity and give me hope of finding You. Your arms remaining open on the cross tell me I can put my trust in becoming rich through that gesture. Your breast wounded by the spear tells me how great is the love that's reserved for me in heaven.

Forgive me when I go off the path. Hold me in those arms of Yours that are open for me on the cross.

—Umiltà of Faenza, *Sermons*—

august 28 🌿

Obedience is born of love and is the cornerstone of faith. She's a queen, and whoever marries her will never know evil, only peace and tranquility. No matter how the sea's turbulent waves pound against her, they can't hurt the soul's marrow.

The soul feels no hatred when she's hurt, because she wants to be respectful to God. She remembers she's been commanded to forgive. She doesn't suffer when her own wishes aren't satisfied because she's made Me—her God—her number one priority. She loves me more than any of her own requests.

In turn, I know how to satisfy the soul's wants, and I can and will satisfy them, always. Obedience is the key to peace.

—Catherine of Siena, *Dialogue*—

august 29 🌿

If you want faith, pray. If you want hope, pray. If you want kindness, pray. If you want poverty, pray. If you want obedience, pray. If you want integrity, pray. If you want humility, pray. If you want gentleness, pray. If you want strength, pray. If you want any virtue, pray.

Like this: Always read the Book of Life, which is the life of the God-Man, Jesus Christ, who lived in poverty, pain, scorn, and true obedience. Don't skim this book. Let it penetrate you while you read it. It'll teach you everything you need to know, no matter your present circumstances. It will fill you with a burning fire that will be your greatest consolation.

And the more you pray, the more you'll be enlightened. As you pray, you'll see God's goodness more deeply. And the deeper and more excellent your spiritual eyesight, the more you'll love.

The more you love, the more joy you'll take in all you see, and the greater your joy, the greater your understanding. Then you'll reach the completeness of Light because you'll understand you can't understand anything at all.

—Angela of Foligno, *Instructions*—

august 30 🌿

When I was beginning to come out of my ecstatic trance, and as soon as I was able to draw a breath, the Lord had me say, "Your mercy, Lord, stretches up to heaven, and Your truth reaches to the clouds. Your justice is like the tallest mountains, and Your judgments are as deep as the deepest canyon. We'll be drunk with the abundance of Your hospitality when You give us much to drink from the flood of Your joy.

"Lord, You're the fountain of light. In Your light we see the Light. Stretch Your mercy out to those who know You and Your justice to those who have honest hearts, just like the psalmist sang." And I thanked God, saying, "Thank You, Lord Jesus Christ, for showing me, Your undeserving servant, these wonderful mysteries."

—Elisabeth of Schönau, *Second Book of Visions*—

august 31 🌿

Peter wrote that God has ransomed us not with gold or silver, but with His own sweet precious blood. Our gentle Savior's love for us is unlimited. God took death on Himself so He could give us the life of grace.

When our gentle Savior saw we were straying from the way of love, His sole desire was to embrace the most shameful death He could have chosen, to restore us to the embrace of God's love. That's amazing! Our Savior saw we'd fallen sick because of our excessive longing for transitory things, but these pass like the wind—either they get away from us or we take leave of them soon enough.

—Catherine of Siena, *Letters*—

september

september 1

God's Soul is the wind rustling plants and leaves,
the dew dancing on the grass,
the rainy breezes making everything to grow.
Just like this, the kindness of a person flows, touching
those dragging burdens of longing.
We should be a breeze helping the homeless,
dew comforting those who are depressed,
the cool, misty air refreshing the exhausted,
and with God's teaching we have got to feed the hungry:

This is how we share God's soul.

—Hildegard of Bingen, *Hymn*—

september 2 ❦

Gentle, loving Knight, You made nothing of Your death, Your life, or Your shame. No, on the cross You battled the death that is our sin, and though death destroyed Your bodily life, Your death destroyed our death.

Love's the reason, you see. The Lord's eye was fixed on nothing but His Father's honor. He wanted nothing more than to make God's wish for us come true, so we could experience God—that's why He created us.

Constantly look into the gentle eye of God's love.

—Catherine of Siena, *Letters*—

september 3 ❦

Imitate God. Remember God is all good, and don't let yourself indulge in pride, envy, schisms, and other sins that fight against the spirit. These lead to decadence.

Instead, be like newborn babies. Be people of integrity. Never be duplicitous. Why? Remember that the Lord said in Leviticus to His loyal friends that they were to be holy because He was holy.

The Lord has blessed you for many years. He's shown you treasure hidden in a field, and you've enjoyed it for such a long time. With your joy you bought God's priceless treasure, the best pearls and gems. Remember that—without a doubt—if you respect these jewels as you should, they'll always stand before the face of God, praying for you and begging for the salvation of your body and soul.

—Elisabeth of Schönau, *Letters*—

september 4 🌿

Remember what Jesus Christ said about celebrity in the Gospel of Luke? The greatest Teacher said that those who humble themselves will be applauded. So be willing to be the least of all. That is true greatness.

If you live every day with a respect for others, God's happy love will become your best friend. May God always give you His best grace. Keep living in God's holy, tender love. Gentle Jesus! Jesus love!

—Catherine of Siena, *Letters*—

september 5 🌿

Each person has a complete nature in the Holy Trinity, and God fashioned it with His own divine hands. However, when we disobeyed God's love, we canceled the Lord's holy efforts on our behalf, and God was forced back within Himself by a trinity of light. But God's love made Him want to restore us with His own feet and hands so we could have great oneness with Him.

This same three-in-one nature also compels God to welcome us with knowledge and holy intimacy, to the extent we are prepared through holiness and true innocence to receive them. When I reflect on the truth that the divine nature now includes bone and flesh, body and soul, I become ecstatic and joyful, far beyond what I deserve.

Only the soul with its flesh is mistress of the house in heaven and sits next to the Eternal Master of the house and is most like Him. There eye reflects eye, spirit flows to spirit, hand touches hand, mouth speaks to mouth, and heart greets heart. This is how the Lord and Master honors the mistress at His side.

—Mechthild of Magdeburg—
The Flowing Light of the Godhead

september 6 🍂

Immeasurable, complete Love! You're really in love with every thing and every person You've made. Although You can't suffer, God, You wanted to reconcile us to You in peace, and the sin we'd done had to be punished.

However, there was no way we ourselves could satisfy the tremendous wrong done against You, Eternal Father. That's why Your love found another way for us. You clothed Your Word, Your Son, in our flesh. Jesus honored You and satisfied Your righteous anger by taking into His own flesh the suffering and punishment intended for us.

198

Knowing this, how can we do anything but surrender ourselves to you? We see how Jesus wrestled death on the cross and let Himself be conquered even as He won. Christ's death conquered death even as His earthly death conquered His earthly life, and that's how Life conquered Death, by utterly destroying it.

Life and Death fought and death was utterly defeated, and God's resurrected Life gives us life. May God set you on fire with love. Gentle Jesus. Gentle Jesus. Jesus, gentle Jesus.

—Catherine of Siena, *Letters*—

september 7 🌿

When I was living through a terrible period of suffering, God revealed Himself to my soul. God showed me then the wounds of His heart and said, "See how they've hurt Me."

And my Soul said: "Lord, why did You suffer such grief? Surely in Your pure prayer in the Garden of Gethsemane, when Your precious drops of blood ran down to the ground, wasn't that sufficient suffering to redeem the whole world?"

"No," he said, "that didn't satisfy My Father because all the poverty, labor, suffering, and humiliation were just knocking at the gate of heaven up to the time when My heart's blood poured onto this earth.

"Heaven was only opened by My blood. Salvation was achieved only by My long sadness."

—Mechthild of Magdeburg—
The Flowing Light of the Godhead

september 8 ❦

Love is always new!
Those who live in Love,
are renewed each day
and through their frequent acts of goodness
are born all over again.

How can anyone stay old in Love's presence?
How can anyone be timid there?

Mature souls always have new wisdom.
They never hesitate to give themselves away to Love
in every new moment.
I call these old people the Rejuvenated.

They become attached to Love.
They look on Love with passion always,
and live.

—Hadewijch, *Poems in Stanzas*—

Praise [God] with the sounding of the trumpet, praise him with the harp and lyre, praise him with tambourine and dancing, praise him with the strings and flute, praise him with the clash of cymbals, praise him with resounding cymbals. Let everything that has breath praise the LORD! (Psalm 150:3–6)

How are we to understand this psalm? Know and love God with an honest mind and pure loyalty. Praise Him with the sound of trumpets. That means—with your ability to reason. When the lost angel and his followers fell into hell, armies of angels loyal to God stood firm in the truth of reason. Their faithful decisions kept them loyal to God then.

Also praise Him with the psaltery of deep devotion, and with the honey notes of the harp. Praise him with the tambourine of suffering and with dancing in thanksgiving. Praise Him with the stringed instruments of human redemption and with the flute of divine protection.

Let every spirit who adores God honor and praise the Lord, for He is the Lord of all. Everyone who wants life should glorify Him who is Life.

—Hildegard of Bingen, *Scivias*—

september 10 🌿

After a bitter tonic a person certainly needs some delicious food. How about good will, humility, and love then?

It's better for a person to be inconsolable following God's will, than for a person to be superficially happy following their own will. God's will is pure. All people who love God intensely in their hearts become outwardly calm, because they know all external effort blocks the spirit within. At such times, the spirit sings within in a beautiful voice transcending every earthly song.

—Mechthild of Magdeburg—
The Flowing Light of the Godhead

september 11 🌿

God says, "Weep now, you who are My servants. Through your compassion and constant, submissive prayer, I want to be merciful to the world. Run along the path of truth—dead to yourselves—so you'll never be scolded for walking slowly. I'll demand more of you now than ever before, because I've revealed My very self to you.

"Be careful not to leave the cell of self-knowledge. In this private place, watch over the treasure I've given you, so you can spend it. This treasure is My true teaching on peace. My teaching is based on the Living Rock, My Son—the gentle Christ Jesus—and it's clothed in the Light that can detect darkness.

"Put on this Light of love. Wear it."

—Catherine of Siena, *Dialogue*—

september 12 ❦

Humility always has a good cry and then forgets petty insults. Remember this. If you want to conquer the devil, arm yourself with humility. Lucifer frantically flees it. When humility is present, Lucifer hides like a snake in a hole. Satan knows that if humility finds him, it immediately snaps him like a fragile thread.

Humility's like the soul, and love's like the body. These two can't be separated from each other. They work together, just as soul and body can't be separated from each other but work together as long as a person lives in the body. So, for the glory of God and your own good health, chase after humility and love. The person who has knowledge in the Holy Spirit and wings of faith should taste, embrace, and receive God's friendly advice in their soul.

—Hildegard of Bingen, *Scivias*—

I'm sick, and I long—I thirst for the health tonic Jesus Himself drank here on earth. When Jesus, God and Man, came into the crib, the tonic was ready for Him. Christ drank so much of it and got so drunk with the fire of love that through the strength of His virtues He endured for every one of us the most intense of sufferings, but Jesus always turned to Goodness and Virtue, never faltering.

I long for His health tonic, which is suffering for love of God. Suffering, however, is bitter, so we grind up a spice called "willingly suffering."

We add a second spice called "patience in suffering," but because it, too, is often bitter, we also grind up the spice called "experiencing holy intimacy," and we add it to the mix because it turns patience sweet and makes our hard work pleasant.

"To persevere for many years in suffering" is another bitter ingredient of this drink, so we also grind up "living with indefatigable joy" and add it to the tonic, to sweeten it.

Dear Lord, if You'd give me this tonic, I could live every day tirelessly, suffering with joy. I'd even stay on earth willingly and decline heaven. That's how intensely I long for this tonic. Give it to me according to Your dear will. Give it to all who desire it for love of You.

—Mechthild of Magdeburg—
The Flowing Light of the Godhead

At the end of Jesus' life, he was stripped naked, scourged at the pillar, dehydrated, and so poor neither the earth nor the wood of the cross offered Him a place to lay His head. God was homeless. Christ had nowhere to rest His head except His own shoulder. That's because Jesus was drunk with love.

The Lord made a bath for us of His blood when His Lamb's body was broken open and blood gushed from every part. Yet—out of this very misery and poverty—God gave you unbelievable wealth. From the narrow wood of the cross, God extended His generosity to everyone, everywhere.

—Catherine of Siena, *Dialogue*—

In my misfortune, I ask You, dear Lord, to come to me as my best friend.

I ask You, Lord, to come as a faithful confessor to a best friend.

I ask You, Lord, to come to me as a loyal brother to a much-loved sister.

I ask You, Lord, to come as a dependable, kind father to a beloved child.

I ask You, dear youthful Jesus, child of the virgin, to come as my most intimate bridegroom, and make my soul rich. It's customary for noble bridegrooms to give their brides a handsome morning gift after the night of the wedding. So take me on the arm of Your love and cover me with the cloak of Your long-valued longing.

—Mechthild of Magdeburg—
The Flowing Light of the Godhead

september 16 ❦

Love said to me, "Who is hurt by the children of pride? Only your neighbors. You injure them when your too-high opinion of yourself leads you to consider that you are superior and ought therefore to look down on others as being beneath you.

"And here's something even worse. If pride finds itself in a position of authority, it becomes the mother of injustice and the creator of all things unkind. Authoritative pride thoroughly enjoys being in control by bullying those under it mercilessly and for no reason."

—Catherine of Siena, *Dialogue*—

september 17 ❦

God is found in praying. Three types of prayer exist, and you can't find God without these. The three types of prayer are physical, mental, and miraculous.

Physical prayer occurs when you speak out loud and genuflect. I never abandon this type of prayer, never, because sometimes when I dedicate myself solely to mental prayer, laziness or sleepiness keeps me from really praying. Then I choose physical prayer because it leads to mental prayer.

Physical prayer should, however, be done alertly. For example, when you say the Lord's Prayer, you should really think about what you're saying. Don't just rush through it. Don't try to hurry and finish like some little old ladies quilting.

Prayer is mental when your meditating on God engages your soul completely and you can think of nothing else. When other thoughts come to mind, the prayer ceases to be mental. Good mental prayer slows the tongue and leaves you speechless.

Miraculous prayer is when God—who gives this gift and fills it with His presence—lifts the soul up so it's stretched beyond its normal limits. Then the soul understands more about God than would otherwise be possible. It knows it can't know, and it knows that what it does know, it can't explain. Everything it sees and feels is miraculous then.

These three forms of prayer will teach you who you are and who God is. And when you know who you are and who God is, you love. And when you love, you want to have what you love. That's the sign of true love. The lover is changed—not in part—but wholly into the Beloved.

—Angela of Foligno, *Instructions*—

september 18 🔥

A person spends a whole day running errands, and going here and there, and doing this and that, and the food in their body is shut in as if in a well-made purse. When the time comes for this person to go to the bathroom, the purse is opened and then shut again, in the most decorous fashion. God does this for us. God comes down to us and meets our humblest needs.

God never despises what He's made, no, nor does He turn His nose up at serving us in the simplest, most natural bodily functions, for love of the soul that He created in His own likeness. Nobody can know how much and how sweetly and how tenderly the Creator loves us.

That's why we're able to persevere in spiritual contemplation because God's immeasurable love for us fills us with endless wonder. That's also why we can respectfully ask from our Lover whatever we want.

—Julian of Norwich, *Revelations*—

september 19 🔥

On the second Sunday of Lent, before Mass, as the procession was starting and the people were singing the Response, "I saw the Lord face-to-face"—a flash of indescribable, wonderful brightness suddenly illuminated my soul. In this divinely revealed light, a Face appeared to me as if it were close to my face, reminding me of what St. Bernard says, "Unmade but making everything, it does not touch the body's eye but makes the heart's face glad. It does not charm by any visible color but with the radiance of love."

In this most excellent vision, Your eyes, shining like the sun, looked right into mine. My dearest, sweetest Friend, how You touched then, not only my soul, but my heart and every part of me—only you know—and as long as I'm alive I'll be Your attentive slave. You showed my soul the priceless joy of absolute tranquility.

—Gertrude the Great, *The Herald of Divine Love*—

september 20 🌿

First, because we fear God and hell's punishments, we swerve to the left, and then—because we love God—we climb up to the right, to a longing for the blessings of heaven. As we go along this path, we put on the strongest armor because we cultivate a good conscience.

The right eye of good conscience looks all around it and decides that lusting for worldly pleasures has absolutely no value and is deadly boring. It prefers to look at the light of truth instead.

—Hildegard of Bingen, *Book of Divine Works*—

september 21 ❦

How clear it is to me now that the soul of someone who trusts in God is priceless, and—because of God's grace—the soul of a loyal person is greater than heaven itself. In the Gospel of John, the Truth said that any person who loves Him, His Father will love, and Jesus would also love us, and that They would come to us and make Their home with us.

As the excellent virgin of virgins carried Jesus physically in her womb, you can also follow in her footprints along the path of poverty and humility. That's how you'll possess the Person who holds all creation together, instead of the transitory things of this world.

How many times do kings and queens allow themselves to be tricked into letting their pride reach the skies and their egos touch the clouds, when in the end they're as forgotten as a pile of cow manure!

—Clare of Assisi, *Letters*—

september 22 ❦

Our Lord revealed to me two conditions necessary for prayer. One is a right attitude. A right attitude prays for God's will to be done, to His glory. The other necessity is a complete trust in God.

Our trust, however, is often incomplete because we doubt God hears us. We don't always think God hears us because we believe we're undeserving and because we often don't feel anything as we pray. Instead, we frequently feel as dry and barren after we've prayed as we felt before we prayed.

But remember—when we feel this way—our foolishness is the cause of our weakness and wrong understanding. I've experienced this myself. Suddenly the Lord brought this truth to my mind, "I'm the ground of your praying. I put your yearnings in your heart. It's my will you should pray for them, and if you pray, why wouldn't you have what you pray for?"

—Julian of Norwich, *Revelations*—

september 23 ❦

God Compares the Soul to Five Things:
You are the beautiful rose among thorns.
You are the bee buzzing in the honey.
You are the excellent flying dove.
You are the beautiful sparkling sun.
You are the full moon in the sky.

I can't turn My eyes away from you!

—Mechthild of Magdeburg—
The Flowing Light of the Godhead

september 24 🌿

Jesus, by meditating on the love of Your heart as You hung on the cross and by contemplating the fountains of mercy flowing from the power of Your amazing love, I've received the oil of gratitude and also ointment for any hardship. Then I was able to exercise this love in a practical manner by caring for others, and that's how—thanks to the omnipotence of Your love—I also receive the bandage of holiness, so all my thoughts, all my words, and all my actions can—in the power of Your love—be focused on You and cling to You.

—Gertrude the Great, *The Herald of Divine Love*—

september 25 🌿

When we sin and remorseful feelings hit, God wants us to remember we are His children. Hurt, upset, or frightened children always run directly to their mother and fling their arms around her, and then they give their mother a hug with all their might. God wants us to do just that. We are to act like the trusting, much-loved children that we are.

Even if it is our own fault we are hurting, God wants us to come to Him and say, "Mother, you are so kind and gentle and sweet, but I've really messed up. Please forgive me. I was unkind and behaved in ways that aren't at all like You. You taught me better, but I messed up; and now I can't change what's happened unless You help me by forgiving me with Your miraculous love."

If we don't feel better all at once, we should remember our Mother is wise. God may allow us to cry for a certain time and to mourn our misbehavior, because God loves us and knows what's best for us. Remember that what God most wants is our trust, as child to mother.

—Julian of Norwich, *Revelations*—

september 26 ❧

Even though sometimes I still feel some little sadness or joy, in my soul there's a chamber where no joy, sadness, good delight, or happiness-over-anything-that's-got-a-name, can enter. This is where the All Good lives in me.

This All Good is not any particular good, and it's so much the *All Good* that there's no other good. In this revelation of God, I discover the whole truth. One time, when I was in that state, God told me, "Daughter of divine wisdom, temple of the Beloved, beloved of the Beloved, daughter of peace, the whole Trinity lives in you. Yes, the complete Truth lives in you. You hold Me, and I hold You, and we rest in each other."

—Angela of Foligno, *Memorial*—

september 27 🌿

Suddenly the Trinity filled my heart with the greatest joy, and I understood heaven will be just that joyful, without end—to all who live there—because the Trinity is God and God is the Trinity. The Trinity is our maker, protector, everlasting lover, and unending joy and happiness, by our Lord Jesus Christ and in our Lord Jesus Christ.

This truth was revealed in the first vision and in all the visions that came after it because where Jesus appears, the blessed Trinity is also there, as I understood it. So I said, "Bless the Lord!" I shouted these words reverently, because I was so astonished by this wonderful truth. I could hardly believe the God who is to be held in such awe would be so familiar with me, a sinful creature.

—Julian of Norwich, *Revelations*—

september 28 🌿

The least of God's poor children, I give thanks to the Lord, because from the day I started living by the monastic rule until today, God's hand has been on me, and I've constantly experienced His arrows in my body. My many long illnesses have bothered not only me, but also the sisters with whom I live in community. May the Lord bless them for their motherly affection towards me in my suffering.

Whenever I was so sick I could control no part of my body except my tongue, I still—and I say this without arrogance—meditated tenaciously on the Psalms. Then, when paralysis stopped even my tongue, my mind satisfied its duty.

It would bore you if I told you of the hardships I've endured because of my illnesses. You know the material possessions of our house are modest. But the Father of orphans, our Lord, is worried about me, and through His grace all my grief turns to joy in my heart. In all things, may God—the Comforter of the humble—be magnified.

—Elisabeth of Schönau, *First Book of Visions*—

september 29 🌢

Knowing how much God loves me, my Soul said to my physical self and to my love of it, "Nothing has quite satisfied you completely up until now, although you've tried everything, haven't you. But, together, we'll come to a haven of unending joy. The peace within you will grow slowly, but it will eventually overflow from me, the Soul, into your body.

"By itself, this peace would be enough to sweeten hell. Before this complete peace comes about fully, however, there's much to do. Let God's light help and comfort you.

"Now, no more words, but action!"

—Catherine of Genoa, *Spiritual Dialogue*—

All the soul's seeking, teaching, prayers to God, and meditations are for this one purpose: to get into the presence of God and become Love, and to live a moral life with the purity that is the signature of true love. Such a soul always considers what it is and what it ought to be, what it possesses and what it lacks.

With its whole attention, and with great yearning and all its strength, the soul tries to keep itself pure and to shun everything that could burden it and slow it down as it works to accomplish spiritual growth. The soul's courage never weakens, and its will never hesitates in seeking, asking, learning, gaining, and keeping everything that can help bring it to Love.

The soul must live in hope.

—Beatrijs of Nazareth, *Seven Manners of Living*—

october

october 1

There are two things I can't criticize enough. The first is that God's kindness is so forgotten in this world. The second is that those who profess to be religious are so lacking in their kindness.

Whenever my human understanding grows dark and I cry to God and find myself criticizing this world, I'm certain the lament in my heart is heard by our Lover. That's how we wake divine love up.

—Mechthild of Magdeburg—
The Flowing Light of the Godhead

october 2 🌿

As our Creator, God the omnipotent is our biological father, and God the omniscient is our biological mother, who together with the love and goodness of the Holy Spirit are all one God and one Lord. We are one with God.

And God is our husband, faithful and true, and we are His much-loved wife and much-adored lady, with whom God is always patient and always gentle, never harsh. That's why God likes to remind us, "I love you, and I know you love Me. And, don't forget, our love will never suffer through divorce."

—Julian of Norwich, *Revelations*—

october 3 🌿

Be kind when meeting hatred.
Be loving in the face of cruelty.
Be pure and not guilty.
Be ready for all you might receive.

Love nothingness.
Flee somethingness.
Stand alone and go to no one.

Never be too busy.
Be free of all things.
You should let the captives go

and imprison those who are free.
Restore the sick
and yet have nothing yourself.

You must drink the water of suffering
and ignite the fire of love with the kindling of virtue:
Then you're living in the true desert.

—Mechthild of Magdeburg—
The Flowing Light of the Godhead

october 4 🔥

I, Caterina, useless servant of Jesus Christ, am the most undeserving of Your daughters because I have had so little hunger for God's honor and have been so little mindful of what God's often asked me to do—to live as dead to my wicked will. I haven't bent my will to the yoke of holy obedience as reverently as I could and should have done.

What an unfortunate soul I am, not to have run with a courageous heart to embrace the cross of my gentlest, dearest Spouse, Christ crucified. No, instead, I've let myself sit down and rest in foolish apathy. Lord, I'm sorry.

The Lord answers, "Dearest children, if you wish to discover and experience the effects of my will, dwell in the cell of your soul."

—Catherine of Siena, *Letters*—

Truth was cross with me.
Fear scolded me.
Shame plagued me.
Sorrow condemned me.
Yearning pulled me home then.
Love led me.
Trust-in-God shielded me.
Pure intention in all good things prepared me,
and my good works all stood up and shouted, "God's Love
made us!"

Mighty God received me then.
God's pure humanity bonded itself to me.
His Holy Spirit cheered me up.

—Mechthild of Magdeburg—
The Flowing Light of the Godhead

God's endless love embraces our human weaknesses that are always ready to offend our Creator. The medicine for our sickness is Love's fire. You can never exhaust this love.

We receive this love as medicine when we see how the standard of the most holy Cross is placed within us. In fact, we're the rock in which this Cross was fixed because neither nails nor wood would have been able to hold the precious, spotless Lamb, unless love and affection had held him there. So when we realize how sweet and precious a medicine we have right here within us, we must never lapse into indifference. Surely we'll stand up instead and dedicate our emotions and desires to God.

We'll feel the self-contempt a sick person has who hates being sick. We'll stretch our hands out for the medicine the Doctor gives then, and we'll love this medicine.

—Catherine of Siena, *Letters*—

october 7 🔥

I've got such a hunger for the heavenly Father, I forget my worries. I'm so thirsty for His Son, all earthly desires vanish. I've got such a need for the Spirit of Them both, it goes beyond the Father's wisdom, which I can't grasp; beyond the Son's suffering, which I can't bear; and beyond the consolation of the Holy Spirit, which I can't receive.

The person who becomes entangled in such longing, clings to God in happy chains forever.

—Mechthild of Magdeburg—
The Flowing Light of the Godhead

God showed me how the marvelous Trinity operates. I saw that the one God has three natures. God is our Father, our Mother, and our Lord.

God, our all-powerful Father, protects us and helps us discover and live out the essence of our kindness, which was given to us—and is ours without beginning—through our creation.

Jesus, our all-knowing and all-wise Mother, nurtures and cares for us, and through Jesus the every need of our good sensual nature is met. The second person of the Trinity is our healing, because Christ is our Mother, Brother, and Liberator.

The awe-inspiring kindness and encouragement of the Holy Spirit, our ever-present Lord, strengthens us daily and prepares us to receive our divine reward for every hardship we've lived through, and these rewards will surely surpass anything we've ever dreamt of or imagined.

—Julian of Norwich, *Revelations*—

Pride is the first sin that begins to chase a person away from God,
and if we don't leave it, lust grows;
and if we don't leave lust, greed grows;

and if we don't leave greed, laziness grows;
and if we don't leave laziness, lying grows;
and if we don't leave lying, perjury grows;
and if we don't leave perjury, anger grows;
and if we don't leave anger, slander grows;
and if we don't leave slander, stubbornness grows;
and if we don't leave stubbornness, hatred grows;
and if we don't leave hatred, vengeance grows;
and if we don't leave vengeance, hopelessness grows;
and if we don't leave hopelessness, insolence grows;
and if we don't leave insolence, shameless arrogance grows;
and if we don't leave arrogance, wrong wisdom grows;
and if we don't leave wrong wisdom, unbelief grows and says,
"It's not at all like they say it is."

Lord, infuse me with Your grace. Then I'll flow from Your love.

> —Mechthild of Magdeburg—
> *The Flowing Light of the Godhead*

october 10 🔥

Once my face was full of light, but now it's dark with depression. I'm so unhappy. I'm sadder than I can say, because I feel abandoned. Lost at sea. My grief is greater even than the largest ocean.

If I could only be given the grace to lift up my eyes and look at God and see myself, my heart would leap like the ocean's waves, but instead, I remember what I've lost, and that painful memory scars me. I obsess over what was meant to be, but never was. I can't stop myself from thinking one sad thought after another, and my heart shatters.

I'm oppressed by sadness. I feel homeless and alien. I'm a foreigner in my own skin.

God, I present myself before You, completely diseased by sin, and beg You to give me absolute well-being.

—Umiltà of Faenza, *Sermons*—

october 11 🕯

Here's what the Father said to His Son, Jesus Christ after He had been crucified on the cross. God welcomed His Son home into divine peace after His earthly agony: "Welcome, My splendid Son! You are Myself. My hand is in Your works, My honor is Your power, My strength is Your struggle, My praise is Your victory, My will is Your resurrection, My wonder is Your ascension, and My rage is Your judgment.

"My Godhead is Your crown; Your humanity is My reconciliation. The Spirit of Us both is one will, one teaching, one strength in all things, endlessly, with no beginning. Your soul is the most intimate bride of Our Three Persons."

Isn't this wonderful? See how marvelously the soul of Christ sparkles in the whole Holy Trinity? How like the amazing flashing of the beautiful sun that no one can see who does not have the wisest, most awesome eyes.

—Mechthild of Magdeburg—
The Flowing Light of the Godhead

october 12 🍂

I love you, O LORD, my strength. The LORD is my rock, my fortress, and my deliverer; my God is my rock, in whom I take refuge. He is my shield and the horn of my salvation, my stronghold. (Psalm 18:1–2)

This psalm reminds us that God—through whom I was created, and through whom I live, and to whom I reach when I complain, and from whom I request all good things, because I know God is mine and I ought to serve Him for the knowledge I have through Him—this God is my helper in all good things because I accomplish my good works through Him.

I also place my hope in God because His grace covers me like a good piece of clothing.

—Hildegard of Bingen, *The Book of the Rewards of Life*—

october 13 🌿

Submit to the yoke of holy agreement. That's how community is made. Show your willingness to obey God by shouldering the burden that God has placed on you, and be joyful in all circumstances.

Sometimes you'll find that you're surrounded by conflict and unfriendly people, but don't let that stop you from giving others your best efforts in honor of God. As much as possible, live in peace with others.

—Catherine of Siena, *Letters*—

october 14 🌿

Anger is the worst fault. It's the heart of the devil. The angry person gnaws away every virtuous grain and devours everything that's germinating.

Anger is a stubborn thief. It gnashes its teeth at people because of their worthy gifts from God. It steals whatever it can snatch.

Anger starts controversy whenever it can. Anger is a dragon burning everything up wherever it goes. In anger, wisdom is unwise, patience strains with impatience, and temperance rushes around without moderation.

Anger is the bitterness vomiting out the goodness and sweetness in God's teachings. It's the murderer dividing body and soul and not allowing them to be together. It's also a hard, immovable rock because it grinds away every good and honest thing. When anger overcomes someone, it overcomes them with great madness, thinking neither about earthly things nor about heavenly things while it shatters another person who was made in God's image.

Anger attracts great torments to itself.

Avoid this sin if you want your soul to live in God. Avoid it so you don't wound your soul seriously. Repent while you can.

—Hildegard of Bingen, *The Book of the Rewards of Life*—

october 15 🌿

Rejoice and be glad in the God who accepted you and made your soul the bride of the King and of the dazzling Lamb who walks before you. Run after your Bridegroom's footsteps, and let the journey be sweet. Don't look to the right or to the left, and you'll come to Him.

The Lamb will lead you up into the upper room of His tent, and you'll eat with God and He with you. In the Bridegroom's tent you'll rejoice with the angels. You'll smell cinnamon and balsam and the sweetest fragrances. Before the throne of God you'll hear beautiful music, too.

There's no more weakness there, and no trouble of any kind to bother you. God offers you this joy. God lives and rules forever and ever. Amen.

—Elisabeth of Schönau, *Letters*—

october 16 🌿

Three things make a person worthy of God's path, and three things cause them to recognize it and enter onto it. First, submit to God and relinquish all your ideas about control. Hold on to God's grace and determine to keep it by forgiving everyone in all things, as far as is humanly possible.

Second, stay on God's path by welcoming all things, except for sin. This will keep your heart open and flexible.

Third, remain on this path by doing all things well for God's honor. That's why I think doing simple things is just as important in God's sight as the highest states of contemplation. Why? Whatever I do for love gives honor to God. It's all one and the same. There's no high or low. But whenever I sin, I step off this path.

—Mechthild of Magdeburg—
The Flowing Light of the Godhead

october 17 🌿

After contemplating the amazing sweetness and compassion Christ has, then—filled with pain—I threw myself onto the floor, stretched out in front of God's wonderful body, and prayed humbly to Him. I asked Christ to give me what He knows I need, and the God of sweetness and gentleness came to me immediately and by His grace gave me His wonderful consolation and such a will to do good, I felt all changed and renewed.

After that, I got back up and knelt in front of the Lord and confessed to Him everything I could think of. I told God all the ways I'd offended Him and promised to change and do better. How extremely kind and wonderful was that love.

—Marguerite d'Oingt, *Page of Meditations*—

october 18 🌿

What wonderful humility!
What amazing poverty!
The King of angels—
Lord of heaven and earth—
is laid in a manger.

That's why a Mirror
hangs from the wood of the cross,
begging those who pass by it
to consider what God has got to say,

"Look! Everyone of you going past, look!
Look in Me and see if there's any suffering
like Mine."

Shout back at Him,
"Pull me to You!
We'll play in the fragrance of God's perfume,
heavenly Spouse!

I'll run and never get tired,
until You bring me into Your wine cellar,
and Your left hand nestles under my head,
and Your right hand hugs me, and we're happy.

"Then You'll kiss me with the best kiss of Your mouth."

—Clare of Assisi, *Letters*—

october 19 🌿

One Sunday, after a serious illness, I was forced to stay in bed. When dawn came, I felt depressed. I complained to myself that my weakness was keeping me from church and from the consolation I receive there.

Then the mother of our Lord said to me, "Just as you're thinking right now how you've never endured greater bodily pain, know, too, that my Son has never given you a better gift than the one this bodily weakness has given your soul the strength to receive well."

Mary's words made me feel better. I began to meditate, and I saw my soul—like wax melting in a hot fire—being put close to the Lord's holy breast, as though to be imprinted with a seal. Suddenly, my soul grew and was pulled into the interior of that treasury where God lives in fullness.

That's how my soul was sealed with the imprint of the splendid, always tranquil Trinity.

—Gertrude the Great, *The Herald of Divine Love*—

Once when I was meditating on the great suffering Christ endured on the cross, I contemplated the nails that—I'd heard said—had driven a little bit of the flesh from His hands and feet into the wood. I wanted to see the bit of Christ's flesh that the nails had driven into the wood. When I saw it, my grief over the pain Christ endured was so great, I could no longer stand. I bent over and sat down. I stretched my arms out on the ground in front of me and lay my head on them.

Then Christ showed me His throat and arms. At that point my grief was changed into such intense joy, I can't describe it. This joy was new, not like all the others. The joy in me was absolutely certain, and the stunning beauty of Christ's throat and neck convinced me that my vision was divine. This beauty persuaded me that I was in God's presence.

I don't know how to describe that brightness and the clarity of my vision. I can't think of anything to compare it to. No color in the world will do, except perhaps the lucidity and brilliance of Christ's body I sometimes see when celebrating the Eucharist.

—Angela of Foligno, *Memorial*—

october 21 🌿

The Lord's angel took me in spirit high up to a place where I could see a spectacular city. Within the golden walls of this city rose an especially splendid tower. Extremely tall, this tower was made of nothing but the purest light. Its brightness was like the brilliance of gold reflecting the sun, and I couldn't look at it for the abundance of shine flashing out from it. Then I realized that the city was not illuminated by the sun or moon or any other heavenly body, but by this tower's amazing brilliance.

An angel was my guide, and this angel explained what my vision meant: "The city you saw is a symbol of the Lord, our Savior. The golden wall is a sign of God's invaluable humanity, and the tower of bright light illuminating the whole city symbolizes the majesty of His divinity, which He allowed to be encompassed by the limits of human nature."

—Elisabeth of Schönau, *Third Book of Visions*—

october 22 🌿

One evening I was kneeling in prayer before going to bed when suddenly a verse came into my head that anyone who loves Jesus will keep His word, and His Father will love her, and They will come to her and make Their home with her, as St. John tells us in his Gospel. Then, within my inner self, my heart of clay felt Your coming, God. I felt Your presence within me.

O how I wish a thousand times over that the ocean would turn into blood and sail over my head, so this sinful earth in which Your inconceivable Majesty stooped to dwell might be overcome by this cleansing flood. Or I wish my heart could be ripped this instant from my body and thrown in pieces into a pile of burning coals! Then it would be purged of impurities. It would become—I won't say a "worthy"—but a less unworthy home for You.

—Gertrude the Great, *The Herald of Divine Love*—

october 23

Kind Christ—You're my only hope—come to me. Don't be slow to visit my heart, which desperately needs Your love. Fill it with divine grace. Join my mind and soul. Make them burn in You who are flame without smoke always, wholly resplendent.

Come to me and bring Your love, gorgeous Fire that makes all things bear fruit. You draw the seeds out of the dry ground and make them grow. Hear me, excellent Sower. My heart only wants the seed of love from You. This seed grows instantly and produces the best fruit.

I beg only love from You. Come then, Jesus, sweet Lover. Don't dawdle!

—Umiltà of Faenza, *Sermons*—

God commands us, "Don't blame yourself for every bad thing that happens to you, and for your every grief. I don't want you to be depressed. Listen to my advice instead. I'm telling you—no matter what you do, no matter how purely you live—you'll have sorrow. That's why you must live a life of humility."

Earth is a prison, this life is penance, and God wants us to rejoice in the remedy, which is this: Our Lord is with us always. That's our remedy. God protects us and leads us into His holistic joy. God wants this joy to be unending, too. God wants to be our happiness here on earth and also our trustworthy way into heaven.

So run to the Lord and be hugged. Touch Him, and be made clean. Cling to Him, and you'll be safe. Our considerate Lord wants us to be as familiar with Him as our hearts can imagine and our souls can hope.

But don't be so careless that you accept this intimacy and forget your good manners. Our Lord is supreme familiarity, but He is as polite as He is familiar. God truly is the best manners.

—Julian of Norwich, *Revelations*—

october 25 🌿

Christ's tasting the bitter vinegar allowed Him to give you the best sweetness. Christ's sadness allowed Him to give you consolation. Christ's nails and cross allowed Him to release you from sin's deadly chains. Christ's servanthood allowed Him to rescue you from slavery to the devil. Christ let Himself be sold so He could ransom you with His own blood. God chose death for Himself to give you life.

—Catherine of Siena, *Dialogue*—

october 26 🌿

The stressed-out Body complains to the lonely Soul: "When will you—with the feathers of your yearning—soar to joyful heights and up to Jesus, your eternal Love? Once there, I'll thank Him that—fragile and undeserving though I am—God came anyway and wanted to be mine when He entered this land of exile and took our humanity on Himself and clothed Himself in it. Keep me innocent in Your kindness until I reach a holy death, and you, dear Soul of mine, leave me."

The Soul answers: "O you dearest prison! I've been bound in you longer than I can remember. Thank you for being obedient to me. Although many times I've been miserable in you, still you've often helped me, too. When you die, your misery will all be over. Your complaining will end, and you'll understand that everything

God did with you was just fine. So stand strong a little while longer. With steady spiritual hands hold on to the sweet hope you have, and don't let go."

Obedience is a sacred bond uniting the soul to God and the body to Jesus and the five senses to the Holy Spirit. The longer it binds, the more the soul loves. The less the body gives itself over to self-absorption, the more beautifully do its works of kindness shine in God's eyes and before people of good will.

—Mechthild of Magdeburg—
The Flowing Light of the Godhead

october 27 🌿

I want to describe a great favor done me not too long ago. I want to tell you of the way God blessed me, because I've noticed that when I listen to someone else tell how the Lord has helped them, I'm better off for a long time afterwards. So I'll tell you my story briefly.

By the grace of God, the holy life Jesus Christ led on earth, His good examples, and His good teachings were written in my heart. In fact, Jesus' sweetness was pressed so firmly into my heart, sometimes God seemed to be within me and holding a closed book in His hand in order to teach me from it.

Sweet Lord, keep on writing on my heart whatever it is You want me to do. Write Your law in my heart. Write Your orders there where they'll never be erased.

—Marguerite d'Oingt, *Page of Meditations*; *Mirror*—

october 28 🌿

There are two strikingly different paths: One is hellish, the other heavenly.

An abundance of material possessions is a capricious guest, while holy poverty is a precious, godly burden.

Pride doesn't realize it's destructive, while constancy is always helpful.

Foolishness loves itself too much, while wisdom's never satisfied with what it learns.

Anger makes a soul utterly dark, while humility is always bright and graceful.

Greed has a loud mouth, while moderation is the unseen, delightful foundation.

Depression is horrible, but true hope in God's goodness will feed your soul.

—Mechthild of Magdeburg—
The Flowing Light of the Godhead

Love says, "The Soul is like an eagle because the Soul flies high, yes, higher than any other bird, because she's feathered with fine love.

"She has the sharpest eyes, too. Without becoming blind, she can look at the sun's beauty and its rays and its brilliance, and she can also fly up to the very tops of cedars and break off a slip of the cedar to plant. This tiny slip will grow tall in its obedience to God.

"The Soul fears nothing. She needs no consoling. She doesn't succumb to temptation. You can take nothing from her because she's secure. Her love runs through all things. She's common to all and asks nothing of anyone because God fills her with pure goodness, which is always polite.

"She's always clearheaded without being sad, and joyful without being self-indulgent. God has written His name in her soul, and the Trinity is right at home there."

—Marguerite Porete, *The Mirror of Simple Souls*—

My Lord Jesus Christ, neither pain, nor fear, nor flattery could ever deflect Your amazing heart away from protecting Your kingdom of truth and fair dealing. You didn't spare Yourself in any way. You bled like a commoner. You died in battle defending these things. That's how You won victory. So let us all praise Your unconquered heart. Amen.

Your revered hands and arms were stronger than Samson's, and in the most wonderful way You patiently endured being nailed to the wood of the cross. May we worship Your arms and hands because they saved us all and deserve everlasting praise and glory. Amen.

Finally, my Lord Jesus Christ, may Your beloved ribs and back be blessed and honored everywhere by all who sweat as they work through spiritual and earthly matters. Your entire life, You worked without stopping, for our salvation. You knew the worst of all pain when You bore our sins on Your back. Amen.

—Birgitta of Sweden, *Prayers*—

october 31 ❧

God is all-strong and all-powerful. Because of that, God gives His friends the ability to do whatever they need to do. If they wanted to lift the whole world with their little finger, they could do it easily.

God is all-wisdom, too, and gives so much of it to His friends, they'll never have to ask for anything because they'll have everything they desire. God is also all-love and gives so much of it to us that we love each other, and what one of us wants, the others want, too.

—Marguerite d'Oingt, *Mirror*—

n o v e m b e r

november 1

No matter how sad the season and silent the birds,
brave hearts enduring pain willingly—
for Love—have no need of sadness.
They know and understand all things instead—
sweetness and cruelty, joy and sorrow—
they know everything that must be lived through for Love's
sake.

Patience.

—Hadewijch, *Poems in Stanzas*—

november 2 🌿

We read in the First Letter of John that the reason the Son of God appeared was to destroy the works of the devil. The great brightness—the Son of God—appeared for humanity's health and salvation. God took on the poverty of a human body but shone in it like a burning star among gray clouds.

God was placed on the winepress, and the best wine was pressed out without the dregs of fermentation because the Cornerstone fell upon the press and made such wine that it produced the greatest aroma of sweetness.

Shining as a splendid human being among the human race, with no hint of sinfulness, the Son of God walked with His warlike foot upon the head of the ancient serpent, destroying all the daggers of the devil's iniquity—full of rage and lust as they were—and utterly disgracing him.

—Hildegard of Bingen, *Scivias*—

november 3 🌿

When on this earth you experience sadness that you've not desired and that you've in no way caused, our Lord sees; and He has this to say to you: "I set your sadness in motion, but not in the way you might think. Look, it's like this. Just as my Father had Me set in motion on earth, so too, whomever I draw to Myself on earth will suffer much pain because of it.

"You must be aware that the more vigorously I draw you towards Me, the nearer you come to Me and My suffering. When you've overcome yourself so well that you consider suffering and consolation equally important, then I'll raise you up into sweetness, and you'll sample what eternal life tastes like."

—Mechthild of Magdeburg—
The Flowing Light of the Godhead

november 4 🌿

Wisdom—omnipotent moving—
embracing this world,
informing everything that is
and everything that has life
in one unending circle.

You have three wings.

The first unfolds and flies through the highest sky.
The second dips down, touching the earth.
The third whirls its way over, under, and through all things.

We praise You, Wisdom, for You are worthy of our praise.

—Hildegard of Bingen, *Book of Divine Works*—

november 5 🔥

Eternal Trinity and supreme God! Your Godhead, Your divine nature, is worth the price of Your Son's blood. Eternal Trinity, You are a deep sea. The more I enter You, the more I discover of You; and the more of You I discover, the more I know to look for You.

God, You are voracious, and in Your depths the soul is satisfied, yet I always remain hungry for You and thirsty for You, Eternal Trinity, longing to see You with the light in Your Light.

As the deer longs for a stream's living water, my soul longs to escape from the prison of my problematic body. I want to see You in truth, absolutely. How long will You hide Your face from my eyes?

—Catherine of Siena, *Dialogue*—

november 6 🔥

The season and the birds are sad,
but winter doesn't have to be melancholy,
because everyone who obeys the Truth
works loyally, listening to
the Beloved, satisfying Him
with works of kindness.

That's the very best kind of surrender.

—Hadewijch, *Poems in Stanzas*—

november 7

One day I was feeling depressed about something absolutely trivial. When the Eucharistic host was offered up, I turned this feeling of melancholy over to God and His eternal praise. Then the Lord drew my soul through the most holy host as if it were a doorway, and God made me rest my head intimately on His chest.

He whispered, "See? In this quiet place you breathe easy. Your troubles disappear. But every time you leave it, bitterness will bother you, and this will be your antidote."

—Gertrude the Great, *The Herald of Divine Love*—

november 8

God, I know that which has no being—sin, I mean—is not in You.

Here's what supreme Peace said about this: "I want you to be a lover of all things because everything I made—everything—is good and perfect and worthy of love. I, supreme Goodness, made them all—all but sin."

So, let us run, run, run along the way of truth!

—Catherine of Siena, *Letters*—

november 9 🌿

In my vision I saw a fire, and in that fire I saw a globe of sparkling flame. That globe of fire was so huge, the whole world was illuminated by it. Its unbelievable brightness showed me that inside God the Father is the mystery of His Only-Begotten, who is the sun of justice made dazzling with the brilliance of God's burning love, and the light of His Only-Begotten is so glorious, every creature is illumined by its clarity. Over this I saw three little torches arranged in such a way that by their fire they hold up the globe lest it fall, and that's the Trinity.

—Hildegard of Bingen, *Scivias*—

november 10 🌿

Till death, be faithful, my dear, to the Spouse to whom
you've promised yourself,
and you'll be crowned by God with the laurels of Life.
Our labor here is brief,
our reward eternal.
Remember this.
Don't let the thrills of this world—
which vanish like dew—
excite you.

Don't let the fake delights of this deceptive world
trick you.
Close your ears to hell's whispers.
Be brave. Resist them.
Smile and endure when things go wrong,
and don't let success go to your head!

Instead, look to Christ, who goes before us,
take up the cross, and follow Him.
Never let the thought of Jesus leave your mind.
Meditate constantly on the mysteries of the cross
and the pain His mother felt standing there below Him.

Pray. Always be alert.

—Clare of Assisi, *Letters*—

november 11 🌿

One evening I lost my temper, and the next morning I felt bad and began to pray at the earliest opportunity, when you, God, appeared to me as a pilgrim. You looked poor and homeless. The sight of You made me feel terrible, and I regretted losing my temper the day before. I started thinking how ugly it was for me to disturb You, the Author of perfect peace and truth, with the chaos of my evil passions, and I wished You'd go away at such moments and leave me alone whenever the enemy tempts me successfully, and I act so contrary to Your kind nature. But Your reply surprised me.

You said, "I want to tell you a story. A sick person leaning on friends hobbled outside to enjoy the sunshine. Suddenly, along came a storm and torrential rain. How would that sick person feel if—drenched through and through—they were then told they had to go back inside, with no hope of ever seeing the clear blue sky again?

"This story shows how I'm overwhelmed by My love for you. I choose to remain by your side during the storms brought on by your sins, and together in the shelter of your humiliation we wait for the clear blue sky of your regret and confession."

—Gertrude the Great, *The Herald of Divine Love*—

november 12 🌿

As for heaven, I guess you've noticed, God put no doors there.
No, God didn't. And don't you wonder why?
It's because whoever wants to enter heaven, does.
That's how God's love works.
All-merciful, standing there with His arms wide open,
God's waiting—this very moment—
to embrace us and take us into His splendid beauty
and kindnesses.

—Catherine of Genoa, *Purgation and Purgatory*—

november 13 🌿

Lord, Eternal Father, I, too—the most undeserving of all
human beings—have flowed out spiritually from Your heart and,
Lord Jesus Christ, I, too, was born in the flesh from Your side.
Lord God and Man, I've been purified by the Spirit of You both.
That's why I—poor unhappy human being—speak:

Heavenly Father, You're my heart.
Jesus Christ, You're my body.
Holy Spirit, You're my breath.
Lord, Holy Trinity, You're my only refuge and my eternal rest!

—Mechthild of Magdeburg—
The Flowing Light of the Godhead

november 14 🌿

Those who follow God and are brave and loyal
will make it through every storm of Love,
because they know for everything there is a season,
the way winter gives way to spring
and so on to the flowers of that season
and then to summer's luscious fruit.

Those with courageous minds
know to say in the middle
of the worst tempest,
"I greet You, Love, with undivided tenderness!
I will be bold and strong,
and I will conquer in Your power
or lose myself in the attempt!"

—Hadewijch, *Poems in Stanzas*—

november 15 🌿

My present joy is looking at and seeing the hand God's showing me with the mark of the nails on it. I love to hear Christ say, "Look what I suffered for you and others." I can't describe the joy that seizes me. I can't be sad about His Passion then. In that moment, my joy comes from seeing this Man and coming to Him.

My joy is fixed in the suffering of my God-Man. Sometimes my soul seems to enter into Christ's side, and this makes me very happy. Moving into Christ's side is so utterly joyful, there's no way I can tell you about it in words. I beg you: don't take your eyes off the suffering God-Man. If you look on Christ, He'll set your whole soul on fire with love.

—Angela of Foligno, *Memorial*; *Instructions*—

november 16 🌿

God asks, "What fruits of the spirit do my servants receive? First, I look on you and give you light. I wake the loud, barking dog of conscience within you. I also make you sensitive to the perfume of virtue, and I give you joy in fellowship.

"Sometimes I allow the world to show you its true colors. I let you feel all sorts of different emotions. I do this so you may know how inconstant this life is, and so you'll be more eager to look for your home in eternal life.

"The eye can't see, the tongue can't describe, and the heart can't imagine how many paths I walk, solely for love. I'll lead you all back to grace so My truth may be realized in you. I want to do this because My love for you can't be measured and also because of your prayers and cravings and sufferings."

—Catherine of Siena, *Dialogue*—

If you need patience, think on Jesus.

Christ is the bedrock of submission, because not one complaint was heard from the Lamb.

Christ is the bedrock of deep humility, because God stooped down to humanity, and the Word stooped to the most embarrassing death of the Cross.

So be patient. Nothing—no situation—is so hard love can't break through it, *even as it makes you stronger*.

—Catherine of Siena, *Letters*—

The Son says to His bride: "You were brought up in a house of poverty and then came into the society of the great. A house of poverty has three qualities: stained walls, polluting smoke, and soot everywhere. But then you were led into a house of beauty without stain. It had warmth without smoke and sweetness without cloying.

"The house of poverty is the world. Its walls are pride, ignoring God, sinfulness, and carelessness. These walls are yellow with stains, because they destroy good works and hide God's face from others. The smoke is the love of this world. It hurts the eyes because it darkens the soul's understanding and makes the soul worry about superfluous matters. And the soot is pleasure. Even if it makes you happy for a little while, it never really satisfies or nourishes you with everlasting goodness.

"From this poor house you were drawn away. You were led by the Holy Spirit to His mansion. The Holy Spirit is in Me, the Son, and I am in Him. He includes you in Himself. God's Spirit is the most pure, the most gorgeous, and the most loyal. He holds everything together.

"So conform yourself to the Master of the house. Follow God by staying pure, humble, and loyal."

—Birgitta of Sweden, *Revelations*—

november 19 🌿

My only-begotten Son is a bridge with three stairs. Two of the stairs are made from the wood of the holy cross. The third step was made when My Son tasted the vinegar's bitterness.

The first step also represents Christ's feet on the cross. God's feet symbolize the affections because our affections direct our souls just as our feet carry our bodies places. My Son's nailed feet are a stair you can climb up to His side, where His inmost heart is. When the soul climbs with the feet of affection and looks with her mind's eye into My Son's open heart, the soul begins to feel the love of her own heart in Christ's complete, ineffable love. (I use the word *complete*, because My Son doesn't love you for the good you can do Him. You can't do the second person of My

Trinity any good because My Son is one with Me.) Then when the soul sees how tremendously she is loved, she overflows with love herself.

—Catherine of Siena, *Dialogue*—

november 20 🍂

God hates all fear because anxiety indicates a lack of trust in God. Fear is a kind of despair. God wants us to drive it out. Our master Teacher wants us to learn how to truly love instead.

—Julian of Norwich, *Revelations*—

The higher you are, the lower you should be. Don't forget that humility is the amazing virtue through which you reach the crown.

—Elisabeth of Schönau, *Letters*—

november 21 🍂

Sweet Christ, I need to talk with You. I need You to tell me what I'm supposed to ask You for. I just don't know.

You're not unaware of the sadness in my heart. Put Your hand on it. You know my roots well. You know how they were planted, how they grew, and how they were disseminated. These roots of mine took my heart and mind, and bound my soul with a chain of love. Jesus, Cultivator of virtues, don't let the root planted in my heart dry out. Help it spread.

The root is the heart's intent. It's led by love to do good. If my root pleases You, Lord, make its branches sprout, so everyone can see the leaves, flowers, and fruit growing and praising Your name. The root is always covered with earth, and it can only be judged by the tree. If good fruit grows, then the root is genuine.

—Umiltà of Faenza, *Sermons*—

november 22 🌿

Any person who has ever burned in the powerful fire of love, knowing God's inimitable intimacy and unique kindness, can never endure the spiritual cooling off that suddenly occurs when their mind wanders into and through any kind of sin.

The lonely soul turns to that person then and through the Holy Spirit invites her back into community by asking, "Dear lover, when will you desire everything I do?"

—Mechthild of Magdeburg—
The Flowing Light of the Godhead

When a storm is over, the weather's fine;
we see this all the time.
So anger and reconciling make Love
enduring.

When Love tests people
in order to help them grow in spirit,
they will go through storms of pain,
followed by reconciliation
and calm weather.

You can always tell when someone is spiritually weathered
because this person boldly shouts,

"Love, I'm all yours!
Only You can make me happy!
Gracious Love, be mine!"

—Hadewijch, *Poems in Stanzas*—

Reason says, "Sweet, profound God, You are the bottomless nature of total humility, and I am puzzled. Please tell me what Love meant when He said all those things about being 'nothing' in God who is all goodness?"

The Soul says, "Reason, even if we do explain these hidden meanings to you, you'll never understand them. Your questions dishonor this book. Many have already understood everything with few words. Your questions, however, make this book too long because of the answers you require. You move along at a snail's pace and reveal this book's message to those students who move along at a snail's pace with you."

Love jumps in with, "Reveals? I think Reason and her students can only doubt and oppose what doesn't seem to be well put, no matter what they may understand of its spiritual meaning."

The Soul counters, "That's true. The only person who can understand these hidden meanings is the person ruled by Love. It's absolutely necessary that the person who understands the spiritual meanings in this book must certainly be dead to themselves and to the world, because no one tastes eternal life if they are not first dead as Christ was on the cross."

—Marguerite Porete, *The Mirror of Simple Souls*—

God answered me, "You've asked, 'But why shouldn't I seek personal praise?' And I'll tell you. No one is good, except Me, God alone, and I am the good in you. So everyone who's good has gotten that goodness from Me. So if you (who are nothing) seek your own praise and not the praise of Me—to whom every good gift belongs—your praise is artificial. You do Me wrong then because I'm the Creator, remember?

"Since everything good that you have comes from Me, you should give Me every praise. Since I, your God, give you everything worldly—strength, health, conscience, intelligence, time, and life—I should be honored. Praise Me, then, for each of these blessings.

"Manage them well. If you manage them poorly, the fault and the ingratitude are yours alone."

That's why you, my Lord, my King, and my God, deserve constant honor, permanent praise, blessing, glory, and infinite thanksgiving. You live and rule with God the Father in union with the Holy Spirit, one God through every age. Amen.

—Birgitta of Sweden, *Revelations*; *Prayers*—

My Best Friend said to me, "God lives in the annihilated soul, but it's such a long road from the sad life to the free life because Willing-Nothing is the lord of such a life. This Willing-Nothing sows the divine seed taken from the heart of divine will, and this seed never fails.

"But the problem is that many people aren't prepared to receive it. I've found many who get lost in their feelings of doing good, but I've found very few gentle, sad souls. I've found even fewer people who are free. These few free souls have one sole will that Love gives them.

"Love gives them one love and one will, and that's how my will becomes Willing-Nothing in them. This special kind of love comes from the One who is singularly fine, and it is created by divine work.

"A soul who loves like this is naked and can't fear in its nudity the serpent who bites, and since God can't increase this soul's joy, her joy is unchanging. It isn't lessened or increased by her work. She does nothing for her own sake. Everything she does, she does for God."

—Marguerite Porete, *The Mirror of Simple Souls*—

november 27 🌿

What can we learn from the Scripture in the Gospel of Luke that says that glory should be given to God in heaven, and on earth may all good-willed people have peace.

Because the Son of God was miraculously made incarnate, humanity shines in the holiest God, and God shines in humanity.

Because of this amazing wonder, we should praise God, who is glorified in heaven by His whole creation. Everyone who receives the will of the Father faithfully and fondly, experiences the peace of salvation on earth. The peace of good will is the will of all the goodness of the Father and His Son, who is God and Man at once. He is our peace.

—Hildegard of Bingen, *Scivias*—

november 28 🌿

Whatever good deeds you do, remember they're really nothing in the presence of divine wisdom. God in His divine goodness doesn't give anything to the soul in exchange for good works or as "payment" for them. No. God gives goodness to the soul because God is Good.

One sole encounter with the ultimate, eternal, ancient, ever-new Goodness is worth more than any good deed any person can ever do. God's being far away from us is really His nearness to us, on an infinite scale.

At home within us, God knows everything that's as far away as possible, and this simultaneous transcendence and immanence unifies our soul with His will. Nothing can interfere with this union. That's why the soul has nothing more to do for God than God does for her, and that's because God *is*, and she isn't. She holds on to nothing of herself in nothingness because He's all-sufficient for Himself: God *is* and she is not.

So all things are taken from her because—before she was born—she didn't exist. Then she gained from God what God possesses, and now she is what God is through the transforming power of love. It's that simple.

—Marguerite Porete, *The Mirror of Simple Souls*—

november 29 🌿

Where the nothingness of God's wisdom is, that's where God will teach you what He is. There God will teach you, the wonderful harmony the loved one and the Beloved live in in each other. God will show you how they penetrate each other so neither can be distinguished from the other.

God will show you they live in one another in completion— mouth in mouth, heart in heart, body in body, soul in soul. One sweet divine Nature flows through them both. They become One through each other, but at the same time they remain two different selves—yes, and they remain that way forever.

—Hadewijch, *Letters*—

Once during Advent I felt really distressed because I felt the Lord had forgotten me. My prayers had lost their usual feeling of passion and devotion. So I turned to God and confessed everything displeasing that I'd ever thought, done, or said, but I still felt guilty, not worthy to take Communion.

Then I realized I'd have to appeal to the endless mercy of my kind Creator. I asked God to teach me what I needed to do next, and He did. I felt the need to take Communion, and did, and the comfort I received made me feel faint.

But then, after all of these and other graces given to me by our good Creator, I went for two years without getting any special word from our Lord. However, I still kept up my good works for my Lord, and because I was obedient, I felt God's love and respect more and more during that very long, dry time.

—Marguerite d'Oingt, *Mirror*—

december

december 1 🌿

I feel real, deep-down awe when I see that the good and gentle Jesus—the One who rules and feeds the whole universe—was born into such great want and need that no one else has ever been as poor as He was. Look, Jesus is born into utter destitution, and His life began in a wanting that would complete our every neediness and feed our every hunger pang. And remember that in the end, Jesus dies poor and naked on the cross so that He might reclothe us and cover our own nakedness.

—Catherine of Siena, *Letters*—

december 2 🔥

I saw with the eyes of my soul that—up above all things—a fire was burning on and on without stopping. This fire had been burning with no beginning, and it will keep on burning without end. This fire is God Eternal, who holds within Himself eternal life and from whom all things have been birthed.

The bright flickerings of the fire are the saints of God because their lives have given Christianity many a fine sparkle. The ever-glowing coals of the fire are all the blessed here on earth who are on fire with heavenly love and who shine as good examples, living lives of good deeds and peace and joy. All those who have grown cold in sin can warm themselves on these coals.

—Mechthild of Magdeburg—
The Flowing Light of the Godhead

december 3 🔥

In self-knowledge you will find the gentle mercy of the Holy Spirit, the aspect of God that gives and is nothing but love. Whatever the Spirit does is done for love. You'll find the Spirit's movement of love within your own soul because our will is nothing but love, and its every affection and movement comes from nothing but love.

And within the cell of your soul, you'll find the whole of God. God gives us such sweetness, renewing, and consoling that—no matter what may happen—we cannot be shaken. So be glad. Be happy!

—Catherine of Siena, *Letters*—

december 4 🌿

Peace has wings capable of flying, one on each side, stretched out and ready to soar. When faced with either tranquility or trouble, Peace flies up to God. She doesn't give in to terror or bitterness; she remains calm and harmonious. By the combined effort of her two wings, she embraces the one God and persists only in serenity, which is not shaken by the uncertainty of good or evil.

Above all, Peace never seeks disagreement or conflict, but only kindness, always.

—Hildegard of Bingen, *Scivias*—

december 5 🌿

God's endless love contradicts the world and upsets all its pretentious meanings. The world seeks glory, honor, pleasure, pride, freedom from suffering, greed, hatred, resentment, and such small-hearted self-centeredness, that no room is left for loving others for God's sake.

But the God-Man chose utter poverty, insults, torment, ridicule, hunger, and thirst. Jesus scorned human glory and honor, always wanting the Father's glory and our salvation. Jesus persevered in true and perfect patience. There was no pride in Jesus, only a balanced humility.

—Catherine of Siena, *Letters*—

december 6 🌿

Heavenly Father, thank You for creating me.
Jesus Christ, thank You for saving me.
Holy Spirit, thank You for making me clean.

Holy Trinity—whole and undivided—remember my days
of trusting in You,
and send me a merciful death
that frees me from all worry.

Into Your capable hands I commend my spirit.

—Mechthild of Magdeburg—
The Flowing Light of the Godhead

december 7 ❧

Do everything you do with a happy trust in God.
Find your rest in Christ tired and crucified on the cross.
Find your joy in the sad and crucified Christ.
Find your joy in suffering.
Graft your heart and everything you want onto the tree of the most holy cross.
Make your home there with Christ crucified.
Make your home in God's wounds.

—Catherine of Siena, *Letters*—

december 8 ❧

The soul that has devoted itself to God journeys along a rarely traveled path that soars. The soul that loves God guides a person's senses just like someone with sight will guide a friend who's blind.

On this path of love the soul experiences true freedom because it lives without inner suffering. How so? Because the soul wants nothing but whatever it is the Lord wants.

The soul that has God as its best friend trusts God, because the soul knows that God always organizes everything for the best.

—Mechthild of Magdeburg—
The Flowing Light of the Godhead

december 9 🌿

We're all in winter's grip,
but even more caught is the person who loves
because they're held by Love's power.

If anyone is bold enough and strong enough
to risk everything in an adventure—
welcome the sweet and the bitter—
they should send Love an invoice.

Then they'll touch Love
with total tenderness.

—Hadewijch, *Poems in Stanzas*—

december 10 🌿

Incomprehensible love! There's no greater love than the one that made God enter flesh in order to make me God. What heartfelt love poured out for me. When You assumed human form, God, You gave Your entire self in order to make me. You let go of nothing in Yourself that would lessen You or Your divinity in any way, but the humility of Your conception makes me pour out these deep, heartfelt words: Incomprehensible One, made known! Uncreated One, made creature! Inconceivable One, conceived! Untouchable One, made human!

—Angela of Foligno, *Instructions*—

december 11 🌿

Lord, let Your love enlighten the eye of my understanding with the light of trusting in You. Help me see Your truth as You reveal it to me. Make my memory big enough to hold Your kindnesses. Set my will on fire in Your love. Let that fire melt my most intimate being and make me bleed with compassion for others.

Then, with my own blood—given for love of Your blood—and with the key of obedience, let me unlock heaven's gate. I ask this for every one of Your creatures, and for the mystic body of the holy Church. I know You loved me even before I was born, and that You love me unspeakably much now. I know You love me!

—Catherine of Siena, *Dialogue*—

december 12 🌿

God is the foundation—the essence, the teaching, the teacher, the end, and the means by which every faithful soul works. God is known and will be known to every soul to whom the Holy Spirit says these truths. I'm positive everyone seeking God will thrive because they're seeking the Truth, and these words are our comfort against sin.

When I first saw that God does everything that's done, I didn't see sin, and I saw all is well. When God did show me sin, He said then, "All will be well." God also said to me, "You won't be overcome," and these words were said adamantly, and I was

275

convinced. They gave me certainty and strength against every tribulation that might come.

God didn't say, "You won't be attacked" or "You won't be overwhelmed" or "You won't be upset" or "You won't be stressed out." No, instead He said, "You won't be overcome." God wants us to pay attention to His words, and always be strong in our certainty—when things are going well and when things are going terribly—God wants us to love Him and delight in Him and trust in Him with all our heart, and all will be well.

—Julian of Norwich, *Revelations*—

december 13 ❧

I greet you, my dear friend, with the love that is God Himself, as we remember with the apostle John how we have known and believed God's love for us. John tells us that God is love, and those who dwell in love live in God, and God in them. With this encouragement in mind, remember that we have to seek everything by means of itself: strength through strength, knowledge through knowledge, riches through riches, love through love, the all through the all, and always like through like. Only this satisfies the Beloved. Nothing else will.

—Hadewijch, *Letters*—

december 14 🕊

Get up, open your eyes, and pattern your life after the unlimited goodness and love God has shown to all creatures. Then you'll know perfect joy of soul, and you won't be so small-hearted that you have no room either for yourself or your neighbors.

Don't forget that the Holy Spirit's law is amazingly different from ours. Imitate St. Paul, who was completely in love with God. Be a servant of affection who bears and proclaims the name of Jesus. St. Paul looked into this Eye and lost himself in it. He was given such a joyful soul that he was willing to be an outcast for the sake of his brothers and sisters.

Above all, the apostle Paul was in love with whatever God was in love with.

—Catherine of Siena, *Letters*—

december 15 🌿

Embrace the impoverished Christ. Think on Him and remember that God let Himself be scorned for you. Look at Him and follow the caring path of His divine-mortal life. Make yourself scorned in this world for Him.

—Clare of Assisi, *Letters*—

O never-ending fire of love! Thank You for giving us Your flesh as food and Your blood as drink. You're the Lamb roasted in the fire of the hottest love for us.

—Catherine of Siena, *Letters*—

december 16 🌿

On a throne in the sky I saw the Lord Jesus Christ sitting as Judge. He looked serene. At His feet sat Mary, and around the throne were an army of angels and an infinite crowd of saints. Below Christ stood a very important-looking religious leader on a high rung of a ladder. The bottom of this ladder connected with the earth, and its top touched the sky.

Suspended between earth and heaven, the religious leader was gesticulating wildly, looking cruel and deceitful, demanding of the Judge:

First Question. "Christ, I want to know. You gave me a mouth, so why can't I say the things that please me?"

Second Question. "You gave me eyes, so why can't I look at things that make me happy?"

Third Question. "You gave me ears, so why can't I listen to whatever I like?"

Fourth Question. "You gave me hands, so why can't I do whatever I want with them?"

Fifth Question. "You gave me feet, so why can't I go wherever I want?"

Christ the Judge responds to the first question. (His own gestures were gentle and dignified.) "Friend, I gave you a mouth so you could speak sensibly about things helpful to your body and soul that bring Me honor."

Christ the Judge responds to the second question. "Second, I gave you eyes to discern evil and run from it, and search out healthy things and hang on to them."

Christ the Judge responds to the third question. "Third, I gave you ears to hear things that are truthful and honest."

Christ the Judge responds to the fourth question. "Fourth, I gave you hands to do things necessary for your body that don't damage your soul."

Christ the Judge responds to the fifth question. "Fifth, I gave you feet so you could move away from the love of the world and worldly pleasures and walk instead towards your soul's rest through love of Me, your Creator and Savior."

—Birgitta of Sweden, *Revelations*—

december 17 ❧

I saw Jesus Christ, so gorgeous no human heart could imagine what I saw. On God's graceful hands and feet were the gracious wounds He suffered because He loves us. From these magnificent wounds poured out a light so great, it was stunning. It was as if all the beauty of God's divinity was shining through it.

Christ's splendid body was so generous and transparent you could clearly see the soul within it. God's body was so generous you could see yourself reflected there in Him more clearly than you could in any mirror. His body was so beautiful you could see the angels and the saints there, too, as if they'd been painted on Him. God's face was so graceful, the angels who've been looking on it since the moment of their creation can't get enough of it. They always want to be looking at Him.

Surely if you would only visualize and consider the beauty and goodness within Christ, you'd love God so much, all other things would seem ugly or bitter. Think how sweet God is, how generous and kind. Christ shares all the good He has with His friends.

—Marguerite d'Oingt, *Mirror*—

december 18 ❧

Don't think that if your mind becomes slightly distracted, then all is lost. Sometimes I've been terribly oppressed by the chaos of my thoughts. Only four years ago I came to understand by experience that thought is not the same thing as understanding. I asked a learned man about this, and he said I was right. This gave me no small satisfaction.

I'd had a hard time grasping why understanding—as one of the soul's powers—was sometimes very timid and flighty and foolish and inexperienced, while thoughts, generally speaking, fly so fast. As I write this, the noises in my head are so loud, I begin to wonder what's going on in it. My head is filled with the blasting of an overflowing, rushing river, and a tree of birds seems to be whistling and singing—not in my ears—but in the upper part of my head.

I wouldn't be surprised if the Lord sent me this problem so that I might understand it better because all this physical chaos doesn't stop me from praying or from saying what I'm writing down now. The tranquility and love in my soul aren't affected by this noise. While my physical mind races on, the mind of my soul remains clear, as do its desires.

—Teresa of Avila, *Interior Castle*—

december 19 ❧

Immediately finish the spiritual work you've already started!
Why wait?
Follow God's path in pure poverty and genuine humility.
Don't be afraid.

God follows through on everything He says,
and everything God does is good.

This same God will shower you with blessings.
God will be your helper and your best friend.
God will always comfort you.
God is our savior and eternal reward,
so we should pray for each other.

That way we can carry each other's love-duty
and satisfy the teachings of Christ
without feeling hassled.

              —Clare of Assisi, *Letters*—

december 20 ❦

Creator God, draw compassion from us.
Christ, draw compassion from us.
Spirit God, draw compassion from us.

       —Hildegard of Bingen, *Book of Divine Works*—

Those who want to be able to listen well to God's speaking
must enclose themselves in great silence.

           —Umiltà of Faenza, *Sermons*—

december 21 🍃

Love, I love You because You're full of joy! You're a Mother nourishing the kindnesses in us as if we are children at Your breast (and we are). You're rich beyond anything I can ever imagine. You're so rich that the soul clothed in You can never be poor. You share Your every gift with us and even give our souls Your beauty because You make us one with You. St. John tells us that God is love, and anyone who lives in love lives in God, and God in them.

—Catherine of Siena, *Letters*—

december 22 🍃

Lord, may my deepest good intentions lead to acts of love. Then the grieving I feel right now can be transformed into comfort and rest. You're the one who said that a woman suffers when she gives birth, but when her child is born, she no longer remembers her suffering because of her new responsibilities and because of her inexpressible joy. Jesus, my friend, You are the highest humility.

Give me a great love tonight. As Your birthday nears, give me rich gifts, and listen to me with Your unending compassion.

—Umiltà of Faenza, *Sermons*—

december 23 🌺

God said, "Consider the gentle, loving Word born in a stable while Mary was on a journey. This baby is showing you pilgrims how you should constantly be born anew in the stable of self-knowledge. There by grace you'll find Me born within your soul.

"See baby Jesus lying between animals? And so poor, Mary had nothing to cover Him with, and it was winter. So Mary kept God's Son warm with the breath of animals and a blanket of hay.

"Now look again. This baby is the fire of Love, but He chose to endure the bitterest cold in His humanity. All the while My Son lived on earth, He chose to suffer."

—Catherine of Siena, *Dialogue*—

december 24 🌺

The mother of Jesus took a coarse gray blanket from Joseph's saddle—the one the donkey had had on his back under the saddle—and she also took the upper part of her shift under which she'd carried our Lord. (The lower part of this shift she tied around her body again.) Then she wrapped the hardy Savior in this blanket and placed her Son gently in the crib.

Immediately, Jesus began crying like a newborn baby does. As long as babies are unable to speak, they never cry except to express a real need. That's why baby Jesus, our Lord, wept then—despite his noble nature—because He was put to bed in a cowshed, for our base sin. Christ wept for all the world, hiding His happiness. Jesus wept for all the world, hiding His power.

—Mechthild of Magdeburg—
The Flowing Light of the Godhead

december 25 🌿

On the day of the Nativity of Jesus Christ, I took the glorious child into my arms spiritually. I carried baby Jesus and kissed Him tenderly in the arms of my heart, from matins until terce, which is about 3 AM until about 9 AM. Then I went to relax a bit, and I thought about sorting out the problems weighing on my heart.

At noon I meditated on how my sweet Lord was tortured for our sins and hung entirely naked on the cross between two thieves. When I came to the point where the faithless deserted Him, I went towards Christ with great respect and took the nails out. Then I put Jesus on my shoulders and took Him down from the cross and put God in the arms of my heart. It seemed to me then that I carried the full-grown, injured Christ as easily as you do a little baby.

—Marguerite d'Oingt, *Letters*—

december 26 🍃

Lord, I give myself to You as a present.
I don't otherwise know what to do
with who I am.
So please let me exchange this weak and fragile self
for Your goodness.
I place it in Your hands.

You're the only one who can hide it in Your love and so rule
over me.
Busy me so much with Your kind Self
I'll have no time or place or inclination for anything or
anyone else.

—Catherine of Genoa, *The Spiritual Dialogue*—

december 27 🍃

It's true, God is our Father, and it's just as true, God is our
Mother. God revealed that truth in everything, and especially in
these sweet words:

"I am He. That means I'm the power and goodness of
fatherhood and the wisdom and the lovingness of motherhood. I
am He. I'm the light and the grace that is all blessed love. I am
He. I'm the Trinity. I am He. I'm the unity. I am He. I am the great
supreme goodness of every created thing. I am He who makes

you love. I am He who makes you long. I am He, the endless satisfying of all true desires."

—Julian of Norwich, *Revelations*—

december 28 ✺

John records in his Gospel that Jesus told His disciples He would come and make His home with them. Christ was born in a manger, as this Gospel announces, and that is why my greatest desire is to see us at home with God, where there is peace and love. Then we will all live lives transformed by God's amazing grace. God came to live with us and wants us to live in Him, and my soul longs for this—for you, my friend, especially, and for everyone else, too.

That's why I beg you: be nailed fast to the cross.

—Catherine of Siena, *Letters*—

december 29 ✺

No matter the time of year or the weather,
anyone making works of kindness their companion
finds themselves face to face
with flowers, joy, summer, and sunshine.

Kind people are always new and on fire with longing.
Winter's bitterness no longer bothers them.

—Hadewijch, *Poems in Stanzas*—

december 30

When a person doesn't love sin, but hates it and loves God, then all is well. However, even those who sincerely love God sometimes sin through weakness or ignorance of will, but they won't fall.

What should you do, then, when you are overcome by weakness and stray off God's path of love for you? Encourage yourself to get up again and look on God because you love your Lord with every ounce of your mighty will.

—Julian of Norwich, *Revelations*—

december 31 🌿

How can I thank You for this immense gift, for defeating darkness, for all Your generous kindness, for the true teaching You give to me? Thank You for Your special grace. You bent yourself to me and listened to my need. You responded to it, Lord. You gave of Yourself, answered the questions of my heart, and made me content. You flood my soul with a splendid light— full of grace—so with that same light I thank You back.

Please clothe me. Dress me in Yourself, Eternal Truth. Then I'll run the course of this mortal life in true submission and in the light of the most holy confidence I place in You. Your Light is once again making my soul drunk! Thanks be to God! Amen.

—Catherine of Siena, *Dialogue*—

acknowledgments

I am very grateful to Bettie W. Sumner, the Inter-Library Loan specialist at Shorter College in Rome, Georgia, for tracking down many obscure, vibrant texts, and therefore making this book possible. I also want to thank Sabrena R. Parton, Dean of the School of Liberal Arts at Shorter College, for her wise leadership. Lil Copan was the sine qua non; her genius for envisioning books before they exist and her sharp editing shaped this devotional. Thank you, Lil.

biographical information

These short biographies reveal the diversity of the medieval women mystics. With life paths as varied as their international backgrounds, these remarkable women resist stereotyping at every turn. Some lived—as you might expect—quietly, but others led lives that would fit more easily into a modern-day soap opera. Some of these mystics were happy in their marriages, some miserable, while others chose not to marry at all. They were rich and poor, erratic and reliable. But each one refused to be marginalized by male-dominated societies, pushy families, war, epidemic, fear, illness, chronic pain, or any other adversity. These women lived well—regardless of their circumstances—by loving God through everything good and not so good. I hope these thumbnail sketches will whet your interest to read more of these medieval women mystics.

Blessed Angela of Foligno (c. 1248–1309). Born in Umbria to a rich family, Angela was beautiful and spirited, even impetuous. She married young and lived a luxurious, pleasure-driven life, but as she said, God brought her back to Him gradually. Foligno is only ten miles south of Assisi, and Angela took the habit of the Third Order of St. Francis. Her followers called her "Mother Angela." She had several sons, and we know from her *Book* that when she was about forty her immediate family (husband, sons, and mother) died. At that point, Angela sold her country villa and gave the revenue to the poor. She probably could read, but it is unlikely that she could write. In any case, this Franciscan tertiary and widow dictated her conversion story to a distant relative and friar, Brother Arnaldo, in *The Book of the Blessed Angela of Foligno*. The first part of her *Book* is the "Memorial," describing her passionate love for the "suffering God-Man." The second part is the "Instructions," containing her teachings. Angela defines prayer as being "where God is found." *2/11, 3/12, 4/3, 5/27, 6/29, 7/22, 7/27, 7/30, 8/7, 8/10, 8/24, 8/29, 9/17, 9/26, 10/20, 11/15, 12/10.*

Beatrijs of Nazareth (1200–1268). Also known as Beatrijs van Tienen (Tirlemont) and Blessed Beatrix, Beatrijs was taught to read by her mother, and she memorized the Psalms when she was five. When she was seven, she left her wealthy, religious, well-educated Belgian family to live with the Beguines. Later she joined the Cistercian nuns at Valle Florida, near Brabant, where she became Prioress in 1236. Beatrijs sometimes wore a girdle of thorns as self-correction. Her *Vita Beatricis* is much admired, and she wrote *Seven Manners of Loving* (*Seven Manieren van Minne*) in Middle Dutch. *8/8, 9/30.*

St. Birgitta of Sweden (1303–1373). Birgitta had her first vision when she was eight. Her mother died when she was twelve, at which time the future founder of the Order of the Most Holy Savior, or "Brigittines," was sent to live with an aunt. A member of the Swedish nobility (as a cousin of King Magnus), Birgitta was married (quite happily) in 1318 to Ulf Gudmarsson, Prince of Nericia. Although the mother of eight children, she was an indefatigable pilgrim. In 1341 Birgitta and Ulf went on pilgrimage to Santiago de Compostela, and at seventy, she was commanded by God to go on a pilgrimage to Jerusalem. Called the "Swedish Joan of Arc," Birgitta—like Hildegard of Bingen—began a career in writing and politics in her forties, after she was widowed in 1344. She wrote *Revelations* and also *The Liber Celestis*. Birgitta's father and husband were both lawyers, and her visions, not surprisingly, have a legal bent. *4/12, 6/1, 10/30, 11/18, 11/25, 12/16.*

St. Catherine of Genoa (1447–1510). Caterinetta Fieschi Adorna was born into the influential Guelph family. After her father's death, her brother married her off in 1463 as a peace offering to an enemy of the Guelph family, the aristocrat, Giuliano Adorno. Her husband quickly proved to be a rake by taking a mistress and getting her pregnant, after which Catherine of Genoa experienced a decade of extreme depression. But in 1473 at Lenten confession, she felt the overwhelming love of God for her, and she decided, "No more world for me! No more sin." She and her reformed husband moved near the Pammatone Hospital and began their work with the sick and poor there. She is known for her long fasts followed by ecstasies. Married lay woman, humanitarian, and mystic, Catherine's quotations and teachings are found in the *Vita*, the *Tratto* (*Purgation and Purgatory*), and the *Dialogo* (*The Spiritual Dialogue*). *2/21, 3/7, 4/18, 5/31, 6/6, 9/29, 11/12, 12/26.*

St. Catherine of Siena (1347–1380). Caterina Benincasa was the twenty-fourth of twenty-five children born to a wool-dyer. At seven she dedicated herself to Christ and at sixteen took the habit of the *Mantellate*, a group of Dominican lay women. At seventeen Catherine was disfigured by smallpox. When she was about twenty-one, she experienced a "mystical espousal" with Christ, convincing her that loving God meant loving and serving one's neighbors. From then on she cared for the very sick and the poor, while she herself was in chronic physical pain. Sometimes she subsisted for prolonged periods on the Host alone, but her engaging spirit was always bright, commonsensical, and spiritually astute. She details a conversation between herself and God in her *Dialogues*. Her rich personality also spilled over into some 382 letters written (dictated) to popes, prostitutes, family members, friends, rulers, and prisoners. Having a passionate, level-headed pastoral theology, Catherine's intensity was said to be "like the wine of Siena—very red."[1] She died in Rome when she was just thirty-three. *1/2, 1/8, 1/10, 1/19, 1/21, 1/23, 2/2, 2/4, 2/8, 2/10, 2/13, 2/15, 2/18, 2/20, 2/23, 2/24, 2/28, 3/3, 3/5, 3/7, 3/9, 3/15, 3/17, 3/19, 3/22, 3/29, 4/4, 4/6, 4/8, 4/9, 4/11, 4/14, 4/20, 4/23, 4/25, 4/27, 4/29, 4/30, 5/3, 5/6, 5/8, 5/13, 5/25, 6/3, 6/8, 6/10, 6/13, 6/15, 6/18, 6/20, 6/23, 7/2, 7/4, 7/5, 7/9, 7/11, 7/13, 7/15, 7/18, 8/1, 8/11, 8/13, 8/15, 8/21, 8/25, 8/28, 8/31, 9/2, 9/4, 9/6, 9/11, 9/14, 9/16, 10/4, 10/6, 10/13, 10/25, 11/5, 11/8, 11/16, 11/17, 11/19, 12/1, 12/3, 12/5, 12/7, 12/11, 12/14, 12/21, 12/23, 12/28, 12/31.*

St. Clare of Assisi (1194–1253). Clare Offreduccio, the eldest daughter of the wealthy Count of Sasso-Rosso, was devoted to prayer even as a child. Hearing St. Francis preach when she was eighteen inspired Clare to devote herself to God, but her family violently opposed her. So Clare fled her home one night in March 1212 and joined the Benedictine nuns of San Paolo, exchanging her fine dress for a coarse tunic. From then on she followed a life of absolute poverty. She experienced poor health most of her adult life. Clare, whose name means "the enlightened one," gave feminine expression to the teachings of St. Francis. She wrote an autobiographical *Testament*, the *Rule of St. Clare*, four letters to St. Agnes of Prague and one to Ermentrude of Bruges. She is co-foundress of the Order of Poor Ladies (or Clares) and was the first Abbess of San Damiano. *1/6, 1/25, 4/16, 6/11, 7/25, 8/19, 9/21, 10/18, 11/10, 12/15, 12/19.*

St. Elisabeth of Schönau (1129–1165). Elisabeth was born thirty-one years after Hildegard of Bingen, and died at the age of thirty-six, fourteen years before her mentor Hildegard would. She and Hildegard corresponded, visited, and knew each other's work. Elisabeth joined a Benedictine monastery at Schönau when she was twelve. She began to have visions when she was twenty-three. They were precipitated by Elisabeth's inner struggle with suicidal depression. Before her visions, she would feel extreme pain and the sensation of suffocating. Her community, consisting of both monks and nuns, supported her prayerfully through these episodes. She also received comforting visions of the Virgin Mary. Elisabeth dictated her visions to her brother Ekbert, a priest in Cologne. Her works include the *First, Second*, and *Third Book of Visions*, as well as *The Book of the Ways of God*,

The Resurrection of the Blessed Virgin, and *The Book of Revelations About the Sacred Company of the Virgins of Cologne*. Elisabeth also recorded her visions in letters to individuals. *2/26, 5/16, 7/24, 7/28, 7/31, 8/23, 8/30, 9/3, 9/28, 10/15, 10/21, 11/20.*

St. Gertrude the Great (1256–1301/02). Also known as Gertrude of Helfta, this mystic was born in Saxony, but nothing is known of her family because she was an orphan (perhaps the love child of some lord). Gertrude appeared at the Cistercian convent of Helfta when she was four. Here she was taught by the twenty-year-old Mechthild of Hackeborn. Gertrude began having visions when she was twenty-six and lived a humble life of service exemplifying the way of a simple Benedictine nun. Her extant teachings are *Legatus Divinae Pietatis* (*The Herald of Divine Love*), *Documenta Spiritualium Exercitionum* (*Teachings of Spiritual Exercises*), and *Liber Specialis Gratiae* (*The Book of Special Grace*). She also collaborated with Mechthild of Hackeborn and another, unnamed nun on *The Herald of Divine Love*, comprised of three books: a vita compiled from anecdotes about Gertrude; *The Memorial of the Abundance of Divine Sweetness*, written by Gertrude herself; and an account of more events from this saint's life. *1/5, 1/27, 1/28, 2/6, 3/1, 3/6, 3/16, 3/24, 4/2, 5/5, 5/17, 5/29, 6/22, 6/26, 8/12, 8/20, 9/19, 9/24, 10/19, 10/22, 11/7, 11/11.*

Hadewijch of Brabant (c.1150–c.1200). Also known as Hadewijch of Antwerp, Hadewijch of Brussels, and Hadewych, this Flemish Beguine was the most significant writer of love mysticism. Her theme is always love (*minne* in old Dutch), and her poetry (*Poems in Stanzas*, *Poems in Couplets*), her *Letters*, and her *Visions* all reflect this theme. Hadewijch's most famous statement is that she wanted "to become God with God." *1/1, 1/14, 1/29, 2/1, 2/3, 2/19, 2/25, 3/14, 5/1, 9/8, 11/1, 11/6, 11/14, 11/23, 11/29, 12/9, 12/13, 12/29.*

St. Hildegard of Bingen (1098–1179). Also known as "Sibyl of the Rhine," Hildegard was a child prodigy born to a wealthy, noble family. She was often sick during her lifetime, perhaps with migraines. Born tenth in her family, she was given to the church as a tithe. She took the habit of St. Benedict, and when she was forty-two, God commanded her, she says, to write down and publish what she had spiritually seen and heard. Her first visionary work, *Scivias* (in Latin), took ten years to write. Hildegard is most remembered for her many hymns, both lyrics and music, as well as for the *Liber vitae meritorum* (*Book of the Rewards of Life*) and *Liber divinorum operum* (*Book of the Divine Works*). She went on preaching tours, acted as an exorcist, founded convents, and wrote books of such merit that they have given her a place among the Patristic Fathers. *1/4, 1/7, 1/11, 1/12, 1/18, 2/12, 3/2, 3/4, 3/18, 3/27, 4/1, 4/22, 5/2, 5/26, 6/6, 6/9, 6/14, 6/27, 7/1, 7/3, 7/6, 7/17, 7/19, 8/5, 8/18, 9/1, 9/9, 9/12, 9/20, 10/12, 10/14, 11/2, 11/4, 11/9, 11/27, 12/4.*

Julian of Norwich (1342–1420). Julian was a Benedictine nun living as an anchoress in Norwich, England. Hers was a tumultuous time. When Julian was born, England was engaged in the One Hundred Years War with France, and twice in her lifetime—once when she was six and again when she was nineteen—the plague halved Norwich's population. Early in May of 1373, the thirty-year-old nun received her first vision. She says it was "shewed" to her. Two versions exist of Julian's "Revelations" or "Shewings," as found in her *Sixteen Revelations of Divine Love.* One was written immediately after the initial vision, and the other (longer text) was written by Julian some twenty years later, after she had had time to ponder what she had seen. Although Julian was indeed a recluse, she was never entirely shut off from the world. She often acted as a counselor, and she made a living by sewing or some other craft. She supported a maid who worked as her liaison with the outside world. *1/3, 1/16, 1/17, 1/20, 1/26, 2/14, 2/16, 2/27, 3/20, 3/25, 4/5, 5/9, 5/19, 5/28, 5/30, 6/2, 6/19, 7/7, 7/14, 7/20, 7/21, 7/23, 8/3, 8/14, 8/16, 9/18, 9/22, 9/25, 9/27, 10/2, 10/8, 10/24, 11/20, 12/12, 12/27, 12/30.*

Margery Kempe (1373–1439). Illiterate, flamboyant, and often unstable, Margery Kempe's personality and focus on God are too large to ignore. She dictated the first memoir by a woman, *The Book of Margery Kempe.* Her "spiritual" decision to withhold physical intimacy from her husband, John, is well-documented in her memoir. Thirty years younger than Julian of Norwich,

Margery went to Julian once for spiritual validation of her frequent emotional outbursts and fits of weeping. *1/31, 2/5, 3/13, 3/30, 5/15, 5/21, 5/24, 6/4.*

Marguerite d'Oingt (c.1260–1310). Born into an affluent Lyonnais family, Marguerite became the fourth prioress of the Carthusian convent of Pelotens (now Poleteins) near Lyons. She began her writing career with the Latin *Pagina meditationum* (*Page of Meditations*) in 1286. In 1294 she completed the *Mirror*, a book written in her native Franco-Provençal. *5/4, 5/11, 7/26, 10/17, 10/27, 10/31, 11/30, 12/17, 12/25.*

Marguerite Porete (c. 1280–1310). Also known as Marguerite of Hainault, Porete is a fourteenth-century French Beguine mystic who wrote the highly original *Mirror of Simple Souls* (*Mirouer des simples ames anienties*). She was burned at the stake on June 1, 1310, in Paris at the Place de Grève. *1/13, 5/20, 6/21, 6/24, 7/29, 8/17, 10/29, 11/24, 11/26, 11/28.*

Mechthild of Hackeborn (1240–1298). The father of Mechthild of Hackeborn was the baron of Hackeborn. Mechthild of Hackeborn entered the house of her older sister, Abbess Gertrude, in Helfta in 1247. Mechthild had a beautiful voice and served many quiet years there as chantress, choir director, and mentor to the younger nuns. Under the forty-year spiritual guidance of her sister, Helfta convent flourished. Mechthild of Hackeborn, Mechthild of Magdeburg, and Gertrude the Great

301

lived there in creative community beginning in 1270. Gertrude the Great wrote of Mechthild of Hackeborn's spiritual experiences in *The Book of Special Grace*. These two collaborated with another, unnamed nun in writing *The Herald of Divine Love*.

Mechthild of Magdeburg (c.1208–c.1282). Mechthild of Magdeburg was born into a noble family of Saxony and lived her life as a Beguine. She began having visions when she was twelve and devoted her life to God at the age of twenty-two. Her *Das fliessende Licht der Gottheit* (*The Flowing Light of the Godhead*) was written in her own northern German dialect. Its seven books include a highly creative mix of genres: stern prophecy, prosaic visions of heaven and hell, criticism of clergy, and courtly love lyrics written to God. Mechthild of Magdeburg is known for her love mysticism. Old and blind, Mechthild came to live at the convent at Helfta in 1270, joining Mechthild of Hackeborn and Gertrude the Great. Mechthild of Magdeburg lived to be at least seventy. *1/9, 1/12, 1/15, 1/22, 1/24, 1/30, 2/7, 2/9, 3/8, 3/10, 3/11, 3/21, 3/23, 3/26, 3/28, 3/31, 4/7, 4/10, 4/13, 4/15, 4/17, 4/21, 4/24, 4/26, 4/28, 5/7, 5/10, 5/12, 5/14, 5/18, 5/22, 6/5, 6/7, 6/12, 6/16, 6/17, 6/28, 6/30, 7/8, 7/10, 7/12, 7/16, 8/4, 8/6, 8/9, 8/22, 8/26, 9/5, 9/7, 9/10, 9/13, 9/15, 9/23, 10/1, 10/3, 10/5, 10/7, 10/9, 10/11, 10/16, 10/26, 10/28, 11/3, 11/13, 11/22, 12/2, 12/6, 12/8, 12/24.*

St. Teresa of Avila (1515–1582). Teresa entered the Carmelite Convent of the Incarnation at Avila in 1535. She was in poor health the last forty-five years of her life, from the age of twenty-one to her death at sixty-six. Her spiritual autobiography is exceptional, as recorded in her books, *Life Written by Herself*, *Relations*, *The Way of Perfection*, and *Interior Castle*. Teresa founded the Convent of Discalced Carmelite Nuns of the Primite Rule of St. Joseph of Avila in 1562. *2/22, 2/29, 4/19, 5/23, 8/2, 12/18.*

St. Umiltà of Faenza (1226–1310). Born "Rosanese" into a wealthy family of Faenza, Umiltà had no desire to marry, but her father died when she was fifteen, and her family's failing finances forced her to do just that. She became a Benedictine nun after her infant children died and her husband contracted what was probably a sexually transmitted disease. Umiltà was a recluse for a time before she began founding new houses for women in Faenza and Florence. She served as the Abbess of Vallombrosen, a reform order in Tuscany with a rule based on the *Rule of Benedict*, but with a greater emphasis on asceticism and penance. She has fifteen surviving Latin "sermons." *2/17, 4/9, 6/25, 8/27, 10/10, 10/23, 11/21, 12/20, 12/22.*

[1]Carol Lee Flinders, *Enduring Grace: Living Portraits of Seven Women Mystics* (New York: HarperCollins Publishers, 1993), 104.

further reading list

Armstrong, Regis J., OFM, Cap., trans. and ed. *Early Documents*. St. Clare of Assisi. New York: Paulist Press, 1988.

Armstrong, Regis J., and I.C. Brady, trans. and ed. *Francis and Clare: Complete Works*. New York: Paulist Press, 1982.

Auclair, Marcelle. *Saint Teresa of Avila*. Petersham, MA: St. Bede's Publications, 1988.

Babinsky, Ellen L., trans. *Marguerite Porete: The Mirror of Simple Souls*. New York: Paulist Press, 1993.

Bilinkoff, Jodi. *The Avila of Saint Teresa*. Ithaca, NY: Cornell University Press, 1989.

Blumenfeld-Kosinski, Renate. *The Writings of Marguerite of Oingt: Medieval Prioress and Mystic*. Newburyport, MA: Focus Information Group, Inc., 1990.

Bouyer, Louis. *The Christian Mystery: From Pagan Myth to Christian Mysticism*. Petersham, MA: St. Bede's Publications, 1995.

Brady, Ignatius, trans. and ed. *Legend and Writings of St. Clare of Assisi*. St. Bonaventure, NY: Franciscan Institute, 1953.

Bynum, Caroline Walker. *Holy Feast and Holy Fast: The Religious Significance of Food to Medieval Women*. Berkeley and Los Angeles: University of California Press, 1987.

Clark, Anne L. *Elisabeth of Schönau: The Complete Works*. New York: Paulist Press, 2000.

Clifton, Lucille. *Blessing the Boats: New and Selected Poems 1988–2000*. New York: BOA Editions, Ltd., 2000.

———. *The Book of Light*. Port Townsend, WA: Copper Canyon Press, 1993.

Cohen, J.M., trans. *The Life of Saint Teresa of Avila by Herself*. London: Penguin Books, 1957.

Colledge, Edmund, OSA, and James Walsh, SJ, trans. *Julian of Norwich: Showings*. New York: Paulist Press, 1978.

Collis, Louise. *Memoirs of a Medieval Woman: The Life and Times of Margery Kempe*. New York: Harper Colophon, 1983.

Davies, Oliver. *Beguine Spirituality: An Anthology*. London: SPCK, 1989.

Egan, Harvey D., ed. *An Anthology of Christian Mysticism*. 2d ed. Collegeville, MN: Liturgical Press, 1996.

Flanagan, Sabina. *Hildegard of Bingen: A Visionary Life*. New York: Routledge, 2003.

———. *Secrets of God: Writings of Hildegard of Bingen*. Boston: Shambhala, 1996.

Flinders, Carol Lee. *Enduring Grace: Living Portraits of Seven Women Mystics*. New York: HarperCollins, 1993.

———, ed. *A Little Book of Women Mystics*. New York: HarperCollins, 1995.

Foster, Kenelm, OP, and Mary John Ronayne, OP, eds. *I, Catherine: Selected Writings of St. Catherine of Siena*. London: Collins, 1980.

Fox, Matthew, ed. *Hildegard of Bingen's Book of Divine Works with Letters and Songs.* Santa Fe: Bear & Co., 1987.

———. *Illuminations of Hildegard of Bingen.* Rochester, VT: Bear & Co., 2002.

Furlong, Monica. *Visions and Longings: Medieval Women Mystics.* Boston: Shambhala, 1996.

Galvani, Christiane Mesch, trans. *Mechthild von Magdeburg, Flowing Light of the Divinity.* New York: Garland Publishing, 1991.

Green, Deirdre. *Gold in the Crucible.* Dorset, England: Element Books, 1989.

Hart, Mother Columba, OSB *Hadewijch: The Complete Works.* New York: Paulist Press, 1980.

Hart, Mother Columba, OSB, and Jane Bishop, trans. *Hildegard of Bingen: Scivias.* New York: Paulist Press, 1990.

Holloway, Julia Bolton, trans. *Julian of Norwich: Showing of Love.* Collegeville, MN: Liturgical Press, 2003.

Hozeski, Bruce W. *Hildegard of Bingen: The Book of the Rewards of Life (Liber Vitae Meritorum).* New York: Garland Publishing, 1994.

Hughes, Serge, trans. *Purgation and Purgatory, The Spiritual Dialogue.* Catherine of Genoa. New York: Paulist Press, 1979.

Jantzen, Grace. *Julian of Norwich, Mystic and Theologian.* New York: Paulist Press, 1987.

Johnston, William M., ed. *Encyclopedia of Monasticism.* 2 vols. Chicago: Fitzroy Dearborn Publishers, 2000.

Kavanaugh, Kieran, OCD, *Teresa of Avila: The Interior Castle*. New York: Paulist Press, 1979.

Kavanaugh, Kieran, OCD, and Otilio Rodrigues, OCD, trans. *Teresa of Avila: The Collected Works*. 3 vols. Washington, DC: Institute of Carmelite Studies, 1980.

Kezel, Albert Ryle, trans. *Birgitta of Sweden*. New York: Paulist Press, 1990.

Knowles, David. *The Nature of Mysticism*. New York: Hawthorn Books, 1966.

Lachance, Paul, trans. *Angela of Foligno: Complete Works*. New York: Paulist Press, 1993.

Lewis, Gertrud Jaron, and Jack Lewis, trans. *Gertrude the Great of Helfta: Spiritual Exercises*. Kalamazoo, MI: Cistercian Publications, 1989.

McAvoy, Jane. *Communion with the Friends of God: Meditations and Prayers from Women Mystics*. St. Louis: Chalice Press, 2001.

McGinn, Bernard. *The Flowering of Mysticism: Men and Women in the New Mysticism (1200–1350)*. Vol. 3 of *The Presence of God: A History of Western Christian Mysticism*. New York: Crossroad Publishing Co., 1998.

Menzies, Lucy, trans. *The Revelations of Mechthild of Magdeburg, or The Flowing Light of the Godhead*. London: Longmans, Green, 1953.

Mooney, Cathy, trans. and ed. *Umiltà of Faenza Sermons*. Newburyport, MA: Focus Library of Medieval Women, 1992.

Mueller, Joan. *Clare of Assisi: The Letters to Agnes*. Collegeville, MN: Liturgical Press, 2003.

Neumann, Hans, ed. *Mechthild von Magdeburg: Das fliessende Licht der Gottheit*. 2 vols. Munich: Artemis, 1992.

The New English Bible with the Apocrypha. New York: Cambridge University Press, 1971.

Noffke, Suzanne, OP, trans. *Catherine of Siena: The Dialogue*. New York: Paulist Press, 1980.

————. *The Letters of St. Catherine of Siena*. Vol. 1. Binghamton, NY: Medieval and Renaissance Texts and Studies, 1988.

Obbard, Elizabeth Ruth, ed. *Medieval Women Mystics: Selected Spiritual Writings*. New York: New City Press, 2002.

Peers, E. Allison, trans. and ed. *St. Teresa of Avila's Interior Castle*. New York: Image Books, Doubleday, 1989.

————. *The Way of Perfection*. New York: Image Books, Doubleday, 1991.

Petroff, Elizabeth Alvilda. *Body and Soul: Essays on Medieval Women and Mysticism*. New York: Oxford University Press, 1994.

————. *Medieval Women's Visionary Literature*. New York: Oxford University Press, 1986.

The Poor Clares of Kenmare, trans. *St. Gertrude the Great*. 1862. Reprint. Rockford, IL: Tan Books and Publishers, Inc., 2002.

Riedel, Ingrid. *Hildegard von Bingen: Prophetin der kosmischen Weisheit*. Stuttgart: Kreuz Verlag, 1994.

Ripley, Mrs. George. *Life and Doctrine of Saint Catherine of Genoa*. New York: Christian Press Association Publishing, 1896.

Ruddick, Sara. *Maternal Thinking: Toward a Politics of Peace*. New York: Ballantine, 1989.

Ruether, Rosemary Radford. *Visionary Women: Three Medieval Mystics*. Minneapolis: Augsburg Fortress, 2002.

Schipperges, Heinrich. *The World of Hildegard of Bingen: Her Life, Times, and Visions*. Collegeville, MN: Liturgical Press, 1998.

Skinner, John, trans. *The Book of Margery Kempe*. New York: Doubleday, 1998.

Steegmann, Mary G., trans. *The Book of Divine Consolation of the Blessed Angela of Foligno*. New York: Cooper Square, 1966.

Szarmach, Paul, ed. *An Introduction to the Medieval Mystics of Europe*. Albany, NY: State University of New York Press, 1984.

Tannen, Deborah. *You Just Don't Understand*. New York: Morrow, 1990.

Thiébaux, Marvelle, trans. *The Writings of Medieval Women: An Anthology*. 2d ed. New York: Garland Publishing, Inc., 1994.

Tobin, Frank, trans. *Mechthild of Magdeburg: The Flowing Light of the Godhead*. New York: Paulist Press, 1998.

———. *Mechthild von Magdeburg: A Medieval Mystic in Modern Eyes*. Columbia, SC: Camden House, 1995.

Underhill, Evelyn. *Practical Mysticism: A Little Book for Normal People*. New York: EP Dutton and Co., 1915.

Wilson, Katharina, trans. *The Dramas of Hrotsvit of Gandersheim*. Saskatoon: Peregrina Press, 1985.

———, ed. *Hrotsvit of Gandersheim: Rara Avis in Saxonia?* Ann Arbor, MI: MARC, 1987.

———. *Medieval Women Writers*. Athens, GA: University of Georgia Press, 1984.

Wilson, Katharina, and Nadia Margolis, eds. *Women in the Middle Ages: An Encyclopedia*. New York: Routledge, 2001.

Windeatt, BA, trans. and ed. *The Book of Margery Kempe*. New York: Penguin, 1986.

Winkworth, Margaret, trans. and ed. *Gertrude of Helfta: The Herald of Divine Love*. New York: Paulist Press, 1993.

ABOUT PARACLETE PRESS

Who We Are

Paraclete Press is an ecumenical publisher of books and recordings on Christian spirituality. Our publishing represents a full expression of Christian belief and practice—from Catholic to Evangelical, from Protestant to Orthodox.

Paraclete Press is the publishing arm of the Community of Jesus, an ecumenical monastic community in the Benedictine tradition. As such, we are uniquely positioned in the marketplace without connection to a large corporation and with informal relationships to many branches and denominations of faith.

We like it best when people buy our books from booksellers, our partners in successfully reaching as wide an audience as possible.

What We Are Doing

Books

Paraclete Press publishes books that show the richness and depth of what it means to be Christian. Although Benedictine spirituality is at the heart of all that we do, we publish books that reflect the Christian experience across many cultures, time periods, and houses of worship.

We publish books that nourish the vibrant life of the church and its people—books about spiritual practice, formation, history, ideas, and customs.

We have several different series of books within Paraclete Press, including the best-selling Living Library series of modernized classic texts; A Voice from the Monastery—giving voice to men and women monastics about what it means to live a spiritual life today; award-winning literary faith fiction; and books that explore Judaism and Islam and discover how these faiths inform Christian thought and practice.

Recordings

From Gregorian chant to contemporary American choral works, our music recordings celebrate the richness of sacred choral music through the centuries. Paraclete is proud to distribute the recordings of the internationaly acclaimed choir Gloriæ Dei Cantores, who have been praised for their "rapt and fathomless spiritual intensity" by *American Record Guide*, and the Gloriæ Dei Cantores Schola, which specializes in the study and performance of Gregorian chant. Paraclete is also the exclusive North American distributor of the recordings of the Monastic Choir of St. Peter's Abbey in Solesmes, France, long considered to be a leading authority on Gregorian chant performance.

Learn more about us at our website:
www.paracletepress.com,
or call us toll-free at 1-800-451-5006.